T0277075

A
GENERAL
REMINISCES
A LIFE UNDER FIRE IN KASHMIR

ADVANCE PRAISE FOR THE BOOK

'Lt Gen. Satish Dua (Retd) is an accomplished soldier-narrator. Starting his military career in the Jammu and Kashmir Light Infantry, he spent the better part of his service in Kashmir—from a young foot soldier to the General Officer Commanding of the Srinagar-based 15 Corps. This rare exposure has given him a valuable insight into the trials and travails of the Kashmiri people, the ground soldiers as well as the socio-politics, militancy and counter-militancy operations in the state. He has been privy to the many impactful events such as India versus West Indies cricket match in Srinagar in 1983, the hanging of Maqbool Bhat in 1984, elections in 1987, the siege of Hazratbal and Charar-i-Sharief and the Kargil War. On the politico-military front, he witnessed, and sometimes oversaw, the raising and the conduct of the Ikhwanis, the Rashtriya Rifle and the Territorial Battalion (Home and Hearth) in the Valley. His story of Nazir Ahmad Wani, an ex-Ikhwani who later joined his regiment and received the Ashok Chakra (Posthumous), the highest peacetime bravery award, is a reflection of the challenges faced by the Kashmiri youth and their changing mindset. Satish Dua's masterly narration culminates with the revocation of Article 370 in August 2019 and its impact.

'*A General Reminisces* is a vivid, first-hand account of the trials and tribulations of the last four decades in Kashmir and what lies ahead for its people now. It is an extremely informative, interesting and very readable book'

—Lt Gen. V.P. Malik,
former Army Chief

'Lieutenant General Satish Dua and I had the privilege of serving together in Kashmir during some of its most tumultuous times. His deep-rooted association with the Jammu and Kashmir Light Infantry, coupled with his extensive tenure in the region, has endowed him with a profound understanding of the complexities of the Kashmir issue and the emotions intertwined with it. In his book, he delves into the sociopolitical and religious dynamics of Kashmir since the early 1980s. He masterfully weaves this narrative with the life journey of a Territorial Army soldier from his regiment. This soldier, Nazir Ahmad Wani, initially associated with terrorists, underwent a profound transformation, ultimately sacrificing his life for his convictions and beliefs. Notably, Wani is the sole Kashmiri recipient of the Ashok Chakra, India's highest gallantry award. This book is a must-read for those seeking a nuanced understanding of the Kashmir narrative, presented in a lucid and engaging manner'

—Gen. D.S. Hooda,
former Army Commander, Northern Command

'Lieutenant General Satish Dua has served extensively in Jammu and Kashmir and also belongs to the Jammu and Kashmir Light Infantry, a regiment that comprises the sons of the soil. During his army career, he was posted to different parts of Jammu and Kashmir, and he ended up being the Corps Commander of Kashmir, a post that I also held some years before him. He has a deep understanding of the local aspects, having served long with Kashmiri soldiers, and has experienced various facets of the J&K state up close, at different levels, including the highest quarters.

'Most stories coming out of Kashmir portray Kashmiris as terrorists. He has encapsulated the patriotism of the Kashmiri sons of the soil. His protagonist is Nazir Ahmad Wani, a rare Kashmiri hero, who started his early life in the ranks of terrorists, but soon made amends by switching sides and joining a bold contra rebel initiative called Ikhwan. He later joined the Territorial Army as a soldier to serve the Indian Army with distinction and was the only Kashmiri to be awarded the highest award for bravery in peacetime, the Ashok Chakra. He won it posthumously, after making the supreme sacrifice for the country.

'Having handled operations of the Ikhwan in South Kashmir in the 1990s, I can easily relate to the author's intricate weaving of the narrative that includes Kashmir's complexities, the life and times of Nazir Ahmad, the growth of the Kashmir imbroglio, the rise of sponsored proxy terror and the evolution of the state response, ending with dilution of Article 370. As someone who has served in Kashmir extensively, I can vouch that the easy flow of the narrative and the anecdotal nature of description will give the reader a comprehensive understanding of different facets of the Kashmir issue and the adroit handling by India'

—Lt Gen. Ata Hasnain,
former Corps Commander, Kashmir

A
GENERAL
REMINISCES

A LIFE UNDER FIRE IN KASHMIR

LT GEN. SATISH DUA

EBURY PRESS

An imprint of Penguin Random House

EBURY PRESS

Ebury Press is an imprint of the Penguin Random House group of
companies whose addresses can be found at global.penguinrandomhouse.com

Published by Penguin Random House India Pvt. Ltd
4th Floor, Capital Tower 1, MG Road,
Gurugram 122 002, Haryana, India

First published in Ebury Press by Penguin Random House India 2024

ISBN 9780670099849

Typeset in Sabon Lt Std by MAP Systems, Bengaluru, India
Printed at Replika Press Pvt. Ltd, India

www.penguin.co.in

Contents

Foreword   ix

Preface: The Nip of a Thorn   xi

Prologue: A Kashmir Ashok Chakra   xv

Chapter 1: Turning Over a Chinar Leaf:
      Early Rumblings in Kashmir   1

Chapter 2: A Hero Is Born   13

Chapter 3: Unrest in Heaven: The Turbulent 1990s   23

Chapter 4: Thorn on a Thorn: The Birth of Ikhwan   33

Chapter 5: Nazir the Ikhwan   45

Chapter 6: The Rashtriya Rifles Wage War on Terror   53

Chapter 7: LoC Watch: Command during
      Perilous Times   59

Chapter 8: The Rise and Rise of Territorial Army
      (Home and Hearth)   69

Chapter 9: Nazir: A Kashmiri and a Soldier   83

Chapter 10: Nearly Went to War Twice   97

Chapter 11: A Decade of Hope   105

Chapter 12: International Peacekeeper: Nazir   111

Chapter 13: The Kashmir Year   117

Chapter 14: Nazir's Saviour Act   129

Chapter 15: Momentous Moments:
            The 'Karara Jawabs'   135
Chapter 16: If You Get There Alive, You Will Live   149
Chapter 17: Nazir's Last Roar   155
Chapter 18: Soldiering Continues   169

Epilogue: Life after Article 370   175
Acknowledgements   185
Glossary of Military Terms   187

Foreword

The Indian Army has remained at the forefront of Counter Insurgency and Counter Terrorism Operations in Jammu and Kashmir: the army can proudly take credit of having handled insurgency in one of the most unforgiving geographical terrains and against hardened terrorists who continue to remain driven by radical ideological beliefs, fully supported by cross-border State-sponsored mechanisms and armed with an array of sophisticated weapons and evolving technologies.

Lt Gen. Satish Dua (Retd) through his book, titled *A General Reminisces: Life Under Fire in Kashmir* has diligently portrayed the sensitivities and intricacies of Counter Terrorist Operations in J&K and highlighted how the innocent youth of Kashmir was being misled by State-sponsored propaganda. Being commissioned in the Jammu and Kashmir Light Infantry and having served extensively in Jammu and Kashmir, he gives a vivid account of how the army was rehabilitating the brainwashed youth of Kashmir to condone the treacherous path of radicalization and terrorism. General Dua offers a befitting tribute to Lance Naik Nazir Ahmad Wani, a national hero, a dauntless soldier, who, despite having been drawn into terrorism in

the early stages of his life, could righteously re-steer his path towards truthfully serving his motherland and his people. He not only could cut the umbilical cord with the terrorists, but also chose to fight against them by joining the bold contra-rebel initiative called 'Ikhwan' and subsequently the Territorial Army. General Dua switched adroitly between two parallel narratives to paint a cogent picture of the Kashmir imbroglio through Nazir's story at the ground level and his own experiences at high levels. I feel that no better narrator could take the reader through the ups and downs of the militancy in Kashmir and how Lance Naik Nazir Ahmad Wani became the first Kashmiri to be posthumously conferred the highest peacetime gallantry medal, the Ashok Chakra, on 26 January 2019.

I compliment Lt Gen. Satish Dua for this splendid narration that encapsulates the sordid saga of militancy in J&K, how the state response was shaped and how the army and the security forces evolved their organization and strategies to counter the insurgency in the region. Shorn of high-sounding issues, this narrative is simple and should make it easy for the reader to grasp the ground realities of the turbulent times in the state.

I wish the book, the editors and Lt Gen. Satish Dua unprecedented success. This effort will go a long way in inspiring generations of Kashmiri youth who can take a life lesson from the heroic story of Lance Naik Nazir Ahmad Wani and several such patriots who have made the supreme sacrifice in the line of duty.

Jai Hind!

(Anil Chauhan)
General
Chief of Defence Staff

Preface

The Nip of a Thorn

Kashmir's is a tale of sharp contrasts. At one point, there was the commonly seen side: through reports of terrorism, stone-pelting, protests and bandhs. There has been another side with hallmarks of patriotism and valour among ordinary Kashmiris that rarely finds media traction. There is a third aspect of family dynasties that have abused the gentle innocence of their people for crass material reasons. In this book, I plan to narrate what happens when all these sides intersect.

I saw Kashmir in all its glory when I joined the army over four decades ago—the stunning landscape, the innately friendly people steeped in *Kashmiriyat*[1] and their Sufi philosophy of life. I also witnessed at close quarters the havoc caused by self-serving leaders, policy miscalculations, other vested interests, Pakistan-sponsored militancy and communal ideologies. There was a cycle of peace and violence with no definite plan to bring sustained normalcy to the state. Understandably, the people paid a disproportionately high price, and vested interests benefited from their misery. I have

---

[1] Kashmiriyat is a fusion of Hindu–Muslim culture, festivals, language, cuisine and clothing. The rishis and Sufis who germinated this concept, promoted an idea of communal harmony, religious tolerance, cultural diversity and peaceful co-existence.

also been through the operational toils with these sons of
the soil, which gave me a valuable insight into the trials and
travails of the people as well as the soldiers.

Interspersed in this are the individual lives of people
like Nazir Ahmad, a Wani who may not be as well-known
as Burhan Wani but who, in 2019, posthumously won an
Ashok Chakra, the topmost military honour for valour in
peacetime. Relevant to my narration is the course of his life,
the duration of which strangely coincided with my years
in service; he started as a terrorist and ended as a highly
decorated soldier. This transition was possible because
of an audacious experiment called Ikhwan, a forum for
rehabilitating militants, which helped the government
control militancy significantly and later transitioned to a
Territorial Army (TA) battalion of the Jammu and Kashmir
Light Infantry (JAKLI) regiment. I was a participant and
witness to this course in history.

I have had extensive experience serving in J&K at all
levels of service, ending as Corps Commander of the Srinagar-
based 15 Corps in 2015–16, when momentous operations,
including the Uri Surgical Strikes, the elimination of Burhan
Wani and its aftermath of unrest, took place.

Ikhwan emerged from a series of logical steps that were
based on experience with the Indian Peace Keeping Force
(IPKF) in Sri Lanka. IPKF did not go so well, quite like how
Afghanistan proved to be a disaster for the powerful and
modern US Army. It was because these formal armies are
trained to fight an identifiable enemy, mostly on a battlefield.
But when an enemy hides in the shadows, exploits the benefits
of surprise and shows a complete lack of concern about their
own lives or collateral damage to the civilian population,
then old military methods need to be reworked. This is a new
generation of warfare, and it needs a new set of strategies.
Ikhwan was born out of this new approach.

During those troubled years, the army worked closely with the civil authorities. This interface not only provided insights into the high levels of integrity and professionalism of many civilian officials, but also into the self-serving impulses of politicians and bureaucrats. I was privy to many glories and frustrations and how they manifested in ordinary life, such as during the 1983 India–West Indies cricket match in Srinagar, the aftermath of the hanging of Maqbool Bhat in 1984, the elections in 1987, the siege of Hazratbal and Charar-i-Sharief and the Kargil War. All these led to gradual measures such as the raising of the Rashtriya Rifles (RR) battalions, the fencing of the line of control (LoC), the raising of Ikhwan, as well as the TA battalion, Home and Hearth (H&H) and inevitably, culminated in the modification of Article 370 in August 2019. This TA battalion also goes by the nickname 'Kashmir Terriers'.

Such a narrative, I feel, should be a tale that lays bare the undercurrents of politics and administration but also serves as an inspiring touchpoint for the youth to learn which pathways are available for their future. Though the controversial Ikhwan programme no longer exists, the way it was operationalized and the role it played in curbing externally supported terrorism will be useful for future generations.

'*Mulle mullale edu*'—use a thorn to remove a thorn, goes an old Tamil proverb.

This book runs along two parallel lines: my assessment of the social, political, security and religious landscape in J&K between the early 1980s and the 2000s, intertwined with the life of a TA soldier who began his life with terrorists but underwent a dramatic transformation and finally laid down his life to defend his beliefs. While my narrative sets the context and explains the developments and major milestones, Nazir's story brings out the toils and bravery of these sons of the soil in particular and RR soldiers in general.

Together, they form a narrative that informs the reader about the start of the insurgency and the sordid saga of terrorism in J&K, as well as the steps taken by the government and the security forces, including the army, to control it.

I hope you enjoy reading it as much as I enjoyed putting it together.

Jai Hind!

Disclaimer: This is not a work of research. It is mostly my impressions of turbulent and ever-changing dynamics over the years and my understanding of them based on the post I held. The story of Nazir Ahmad Wani has been put together by interviewing his family, friends, superiors and colleagues. The account of Nazir's childhood has been partly fictionalized to bring out relevant aspects, and a couple of names have been changed due to security reasons.

Prologue

A Kashmir Ashok Chakra

The 2019 Republic Day parade will always be one of the most memorable ones for me, though I was watching it on TV for the first time, having hung up my boots three months earlier after thirty-nine years of service in the Jammu and Kashmir Light Infantry Regiment (JAKLI). One of the most decorated regiments of the Indian Army, the JAKLI draws its soldiers locally from J&K and has a mix of Dogra, Muslims, Sikhs and Buddhists.

The President had arrived, accompanied by the horse-mounted President's Bodyguards (PBG), the oldest regiment of the Indian Army in their signature red uniforms, and had been escorted up the dais. It was the signal for the ceremony to begin. The first order of business was, as always, the announcement of gallantry awards. The announcer started the day's proceedings: 'Lance Naik Nazir Ahmad Wani, Jammu and Kashmir Light Infantry, 34 Battalion Rashtriya Rifles (Posthumous).' The cameras swung to focus on his young widow, Mahajabeen, and the weather-beaten face of his mother, Raja Begum, both seated in the front row. They started walking up the dais, escorted by Subedar Major (Honorary Captain) Daleep Singh, originally from my own battalion.

As they both reached the dais, the President stood up and greeted them with folded hands. The Subedar Major saluted, and the ladies gracefully reciprocated with joined palms. It was a sombre moment. The announcer read out the complete citation of the departed hero in Hindi, giving a gist of his brave act and summarizing his gallant service: 'Despite being severely wounded, Lance Naik Nazir eliminated the terrorist. Showing utter disregard for his injury, Lance Naik Nazir continued to engage the remaining terrorists with the same ferocity and audacity. He injured yet another terrorist at close range but was hit again and succumbed to his injuries. For displaying unparalleled bravery and supreme sacrifice in the line of duty, Lance Naik Nazir Ahmad Wani, Sena Medal**[2] is awarded the Ashok Chakra posthumously.' My heart swelled with pride. The Ashok Chakra is the highest peacetime honour for gallantry and is equivalent to the Param Vir Chakra, the highest wartime decoration for displaying distinguished acts of valour on the battlefield.

The visuals on TV were overwhelming. The suffused light of a January morning reflected on all the faces. The President handed over the scroll and citation to Raja Begum and the young Mahajabeen and they accepted them with calm dignity. There were no tears in their eyes, but perhaps there wasn't a single dry eye in the crowd or among the millions of viewers watching on TV. It was so moving.

For me, the feeling of pride was on many fronts. It was the first time that a Kashmiri son of the soil had been awarded the Ashok Chakra. But accentuating it further was what others did not know—he had begun his life as a terrorist but rose from the ashes of that life to make a career that ended in the supreme sacrifice for a cause he had come to embrace with passion. His transition from a terrorist to a

---

[2] Lance Naik Nazir Ahmad Wani had already been awarded the gallantry medal of Sena Medal twice. In the army, it is written as Sena Medal**. The reader will be able to read the stories of these operations as and when they appear in the book.

soldier in the Indian Army was an important milestone in an audacious step by the army called the Ikhwan programme. Ikhwan, meaning brotherhood in Arabic, turned many such young men from a life of violence and despair to something purposeful and productive.

Nazir Wani died young. His lifespan was, in fact, a little shorter than my service in the army, in the same regiment, the JAKLI. I started as a second lieutenant soon before he was even born. And he lost his life less than four weeks after I had retired. While the army and the government would make sure that his family would be provided with the financial and educational resources to lead a normal life, it was only a consolation. There will always be sadness in my heart over the fact that he died so young.

Chapter 1

Turning Over a Chinar Leaf: Early Rumblings in Kashmir

On graduating from the Indian Military Academy (IMA) in December 1979, I was commissioned as a second lieutenant into the JAKLI, which was a matter of great joy. Who would not like to spend a significant part of one's professional life in and connected with Kashmir, a state so beautiful and a social fabric so steeped in Sufi culture and traditions?

I was fortunate to be commissioned into a regiment that was raised as a volunteer force. During the attacks by invaders assisted by the Pakistan Army in Kashmir in 1947–48, several volunteer groups rose up in self-defence all over J&K. Later, all of them were grouped together as a paramilitary force called the Jammu and Kashmir Militia (J&K Militia). It was only in 1972 that it was made part of the army.

All infantry officers report to their regimental centres for two weeks of familiarization and orientation before joining their battalions. Most training centres are located in the region the troops hail from; hence, one also starts with first-hand exposure to the region and its characteristics.

I could not get enough of my first exposure to the snow and the warmth of the people we met all along the trip. It was January, and the tourist spots were virtually vacant since, in those days, winter tourism was not popular in Kashmir. We made a day trip each to Gulmarg and Pahalgam. While we could not see much because everything was buried under snow, I still recall the chat with a group of shy, rosy-cheeked children all clad in *phirans*—a loose overcoat slipped over the head—and carrying *kangris*—a small basket tucked inside the overcoat with glowing coal embers for warmth, like a personal, mobile fireplace. Effective, certainly, but one that

I could never muster the confidence to carry. The children were very happy to engage with us, and their parents would watch with amused smiles as we clicked pictures with them.

But this life was too good to last. A couple of evenings later, while we were walking through the shops at Lal Chowk, the town centre, my friend asked a woman shopkeeper for the score as she was listening to the commentary of an India–Pakistan cricket test match on her radio. It was nearing its end when we left our rooms, and the match was going in our favour. She adjusted the kangri in her phiran and said, '*Hara diya na, tumhare India ne* [Your India has defeated us].' We laughed spontaneously, rejoicing at India's victory. But that seemed to annoy her more. 'Your India', not 'our India!' This was my first brush with this sentiment. We discussed this over a drink that evening, but soon forgot about it.

My two weeks in Kashmir went by quickly, but I knew I was destined to return again and again. I knew it was destined to become my second home, my *karambhoomi*. I would also see it change over the years, and sadly, for the worse . . .

After my assignments in Sikkim, Meerut and Jalandhar, I was back in Kashmir, posted at Kupwara in 1983. Deployed and working in an operational area, rural countryside and remote areas and villages on the line of control (LoC) in Kupwara on the one hand, and frequent forays into Srinagar city on the other, I gained a good understanding of Kashmir, its culture and traditions, and more importantly, the Kashmiri people and, not to overlook, the Kashmiriyat. My tenure at Kupwara helped me experience the dynamics of the LoC, which had only been a theoretical lesson for me until then. I was not 'bored' or 'fed up' with the loneliness, contrary to what I often heard from several experienced officers. I quite liked walking long distances to reach the posts through beautiful nature trails, pine woods and snow in the winter. Being extremely physically fit, I always looked forward to undertaking long-range patrolling or any such assignments that took me to new places and gave me the chance to meet new people or soldiers. All these exchanges were normally very pleasant, and the hospitality of the local residents had to be experienced to be believed. Interacting with the JAKLI soldiers, serving and retired, in every village enriched my experience even more.

A post on the LoC is a group of bunkers constructed at a vantage point in a manner that can guard over a large adjoining area to ensure that no encroachment takes place. Why is this a worry? Well, the LoC is not an international border accepted and ratified by the parliaments or equivalents of both countries; the LoC is exactly as the name suggests. Because of this vagueness, you have to man it physically to control your area. To do this, you need posts and bunkers. Pakistan has a similar set-up right opposite ours. It is from these posts that they have exchanged deadly fire over years, and it is through gaps between posts that the other side infiltrates terrorists. This also leads to encounters between the Indian Army and terrorists.

Those days were fairly peaceful. There was no infiltration and almost no firing across the LoC. In fact, we would even interact with soldiers on the other side at times, especially when locals approached us as their cattle inadvertently strayed across. They would shout across and even ask for sugar sometimes, as they would be given gur, or jaggery, in their tea rations. I once shouted out an 'Eid Mubarak' greeting to a Pakistan Army Junior Commissioned Officer (JCO) on the opposite post, and he asked me, '*Saab agar main aapko sevaiyyan doon, toh aap khayenge? Haan, main aapke samne usme se do chamach kha loonga* [If I give you sweet vermicelli (a traditional dessert made on Eid), will you eat it? I will eat a spoonful of it in front of you].' (To show that it wasn't laced with poison or anything harmful.) Maj. Yashpal

Singh, the Company Commander, replied spontaneously that
we would eat it happily without his reassuring step of having
to prove it to us. Strangely, from military to military, we are
brothers in arms, and not surprisingly, we find it easy to talk
to each other. It takes my mind back to the camaraderie and
brotherhood between the battalions of a regiment. Once,
a JAKLI soldier from another battalion who belonged to a
village nearby came to see me. He had come on leave to get
married. He wanted to buy some items from our unit canteen,
including rum. I assured him of all my help. We already had
a supply line through porters to our post near his village. So,
getting his stuff there was a big help for him. He invited me to
his wedding, and it was my first time at a Kashmiri wedding.
One of his elders, who was also a retired JAKLI soldier, kept
explaining the proceedings to me, and I found many of the
practices very interesting. While there were no Hindus in that
village, there were a few Hindu men from Kupwara town
(they call it city, though) who were friends and acquaintances
of the family. They were cooking chicken separately on an
open *chullah* (earthen stove). My interpreter explained that
Hindus are given chicken or goat to be cooked as per Hindu
customs since traditionally, the way of slaughter is different,
and the reverse would take place at a Hindu wedding for
Muslims. That was my first lesson in Kashmiriyat.

I also availed myself of every possible opportunity to
accompany Maj. R.K. Singh, a senior Company Commander,
on his Royal Enfield Bullet 350cc motorcycle for a drive
towards Lolab Valley, not far from our location. It is one of
the most beautiful valleys that I have ever seen in my life.
You could stop anywhere, and it was a picnic spot, one better
than the other. I particularly remember a small village called
Chandigam, where one encountered two interesting things.
There was a *chashma* (pond) dedicated to a Hindu deity called
Chandi Mata and a temple called Chandiga Mata Temple.

There were a few Kashmiri Pandit families. It was also a much sought-after destination for government officials while visiting this area, and there were three guest houses, beautiful huts that dated back to the mid-nineteenth century. Prime Minister Indira Gandhi and her husband stayed there after their wedding in 1942. She visited the place twice later, once in 1957 with Dr Karan Singh and again in 1974. Since then, this hut has been known as Indira Hut. These were the times when peace prevailed, which made the glorious landscape the very definition of heaven on earth.

While I experienced some serenity, there were also a few rather jarring moments. It was the day after my twenty-fifth birthday. A one-day international match between India and the West Indies was played at the Sher-i-Kashmir stadium in Srinagar on 13 October 1983. India had become the unexpected champion of the 1983 Prudential World Cup in London when it defeated the West Indies by a respectable 43 runs. Surprisingly, during the match in Srinagar, the Indian team was constantly booed by the crowds. The situation worsened during the lunch break when some people invaded the ground and damaged the wicket, although not seriously enough to halt the game. Poor lighting stopped play, and the West Indies won by 28 runs. Sunil Gavaskar later wrote in his book *Runs 'n' Ruins*: 'Being hooted at after a defeat is understandable, but this was incredible. Moreover, there were many in the crowd shouting pro-Pakistan slogans, which confounded us because we were playing the West Indies and not Pakistan.' He went on to say: 'I don't think the Indian players were really upset by the behaviour of the crowd. They were stunned and could not understand the crowd's reaction as they had come to the ground as the World Champions.'

While normalcy prevailed most days in most places, there were some trouble spots where our standing orders prohibited military vehicles from going through. One such trouble spot was Sopore, the town that was invaded by the Pakistani army's tribal *razakars*[3] in October 1947 and where anti-India sentiment has been externally encouraged since. While driving from Kupwara to Srinagar, one had to go via Baramulla, which is a longer route. As brought out earlier, when the invaders raided J&K in 1947, assisted by the Pakistan Army, several volunteer groups of patriotic Indian citizens rose to resist them in different parts of the state. These were later grouped to form the J&K Militia, which was much later turned into a regular regiment of the Indian Army. My battalion was raised as Border Scouts in Poonch.

But in hindsight, these questions would be asked often: were we as a nation not perceptive enough to grasp the undercurrents? Did our intelligence agencies not read the tea leaves correctly? Or should I say tea leaves used in kahwa?

These were only isolated incidents in my mind, and I felt only a little unease since I was experiencing a completely different treatment from the people I was frequently interacting with throughout the state. The political landscape was changing. Sheikh Abdullah had died in September 1982, but his son Farooq Abdullah had been appointed president of the National Conference in August 1981. He was a practising doctor in the UK and was married to a British woman named Molly, who, I gather, was a nurse. He was considered a liberal with a good relationship with the Nehru–Gandhi family.

As a young captain, I had little interest in politics, but all of us young officers would discuss this handsome doctor who drove around town on his Yezdi motorcycle. I could relate to it, as I'd once been the proud owner of a second-hand Yezdi myself. The National Conference fought the elections under Farooq Abdullah's leadership in 1983 and formed a government with the help of the Congress. There were a lot of political

---

[3] Razakars are paramilitary forces. Pakistan Army used the tribals as a militia to invade Kashmir in October 1947.

manoeuvres that I didn't fully understand as a young captain, but there was a lot of discussion among us about tussles between the political parties and within the National Conference. I heard about the infighting within the party between Farooq and his brother-in-law, G.M. Shah, who defected with twelve MLAs and became chief minister with the help of the Congress party.

One incident, however, stayed with me. Maqbool Bhat, a terrorist, was hanged in Tihar Jail on 11 February 1984, and his body was buried there itself. He belonged to Trehgam originally but had migrated to Pakistan. Trehgam is 20 km west of Kupwara, towards Tangdhar. He was instrumental in setting up a terrorist organization called the National Liberation Front (NLF), which was involved in a few high-profile hijackings and killings. This, I gather, was the first militant organization in Kashmir and, in a way, the forerunner of the Jammu and Kashmir Liberation Front (JKLF). Maqbool Bhat's hanging and his body not being returned to Kashmir caused some unrest in the Valley. This is the first brush I had with the sense of alienation among a segment of the local population.

In September 1984, I participated in a High Altitude Jonga Rally under the code name of Exercise ROHTANG. We drove Jongas from Pathankot to Ladakh over Rohtang Pass to Pangaong Tso Lake, along the Indus River to Leh to Kargil to Srinagar. It was a gruelling week, but I enjoyed it very much. A challenging route now too, the roads were even less developed then. However, it gave a good idea of the terrain and the geography of the places where the Chinese Army adventurism took place in the summer of 2020, and of the flash points along the Pangong Tso Lake. Then I realized that the population in Ladakh was very patriotic and there were no undercurrents of anti-India sentiment as in Kashmir. Now, after dilution of Article 370 in 2019, Ladakh is a separate union territory.

In November 1984, I was posted as commando instructor at the Infantry School in Belgaum, Karnataka, and I was away until February 1987, when I was posted to Jammu. It was at a time when the state was preparing for elections.

When Prime Minister (PM) Rajiv Gandhi visited Jammu, I was standing with some of our soldiers on the road close to the Usman Club to catch a glimpse of the young PM. He was a handsome man who brought a new ethic to the muddied political landscape. The early days were good, as there was enthusiasm in the way the young and progressive PM went about solving several regional problems, such as those in Punjab, Assam and Mizoram.

The elections held in March 1987 retained Farooq Abdullah as chief minister. There were several allegations of rigging, and it is widely perceived to have led to the insurgency in J&K and the exodus of lakhs of Kashmiri Pandits.[4,5]

One particular election result merits a mention. In the Amira Kadal constituency of downtown Srinagar, Muslim United Front's (MUF) Syed Mohammed Yusuf Shah lost the seat. His supporters protested that the elections were rigged. He left politics in protest and formed a terror *tanzeem* (organization) called Hizbul Mujahideen (HM), which means the Army of the Righteous. Did Muhammad Yusuf Shah become Syed Salahuddin, the Supreme Commander of and the face of Kashmir's armed resistance, just because the elections he fought under the Indian Constitution in

---

[4] Sushim Mukul, 'When Guns Got to Kashmir Valley After Rigged Polls of 1987', *India Today*, 19 April 2024, https://www.indiatoday.in/history-of-it/story/jammu-and-kashmir-1987-assembly-election-pm-modi-lok-sabha-jknc-farooq-abdullah-terrorism-militancy-valley-jklf-2525956-2024-04-19.

[5] Hakeem Irfan Rashid, 'Dacoits of 1987, Who Rigged Elections Responsible for Filling Graveyards in Kashmir: Sajad Lone', *Economic Times*, 17 November 2022, https://economictimes.indiatimes.com/news/politics-and-nation/dacoits-of-1987-who-rigged-elections-responsible-for-filling-graveyards-in-kashmir-sajad-lone/articleshow/95571046.cms?from=mdr.

1987 were allegedly rigged? Or was that only a trigger? This question has become part of J&K politics and the struggle for power between the J&K People's Democratic Party (PDP) and the National Conference on the one hand, and the dynamic between the state and the Centre on the other.

A cycle of violence and protests started, steadily rising in tempo. In 1989, parliamentary elections were held, which saw a low turnout. In January 1990, the Farooq Abdullah government was dismissed, and Governor's Rule was imposed. The 1990s was a turbulent decade, to say the least. Syed Salahuddin formed HM, an indigenous militant outfit, with active support from Pakistan. It served a dual purpose for Pakistan, namely, to marginalize the JKLF and to prop up local youth in this jihad for greater legitimacy in the eyes of international bodies.

Chapter 2

A Hero Is Born

Soon after I joined as a soldier of the Jammu and Kashmir Light Infantry Regiment (JAKLI) in 1980, another soldier was born in the south of Kashmir, in the Cheki hamlet of a small village called Ashmuji in Kulgam district, the very same year.

He was the firstborn in the family of Sonuallah, a humble farmer who also ran a small dhaba. Sonuallah and his wife, Raja Begum, named the boy Nazir—Arabic for administrator—and had dreams of educating him well so they could all have a secure future. But they also expanded the family with three more boys in quick succession. The income that Sounallah earned from the farm and the dhaba was not enough to make ends meet.

Nazir's early years were part of a peaceful, slow-paced life. Later, he would recall three incidents that left a deep impact on his young mind.

The first was his Kashmiri Pandit teacher at school, Pandit Shubhanji, whom everyone called Bobaji. There were hardly any Hindu students because there was practically no Hindu population in their village. But Bobaji made a profound impact on Nazir. One day, during the holy month of Ramzan, Nazir asked him, 'Masterji, aap roza rakhte hain [Sir, do you fast]?' When Bobaji answered in the negative, Nazir asked with childish bluntness, 'Toh aap kafir hain [So you are an infidel]?' Bobaji smiled at his pupil and said, 'Main Navratra ka upwaas rakhta hoon [I fast during the Hindu holy days of Navratra].' The teacher then explained patiently how different religions had different customs. It was like using different modes of transport to reach the same destination. 'Jab tum shahar jaate ho toh koi cycle se jaata hai, koi bus

15

par aur koi paidal. Akhir mein sab shahar pahunch jaate hain
[You could travel to the city on a bicycle, by bus or on foot.
But the destination is the same].'

Nazir was intrigued: '*Toh aap namaz bhi nahin padte* [So,
you don't even say the customary Islamic prayers]?' By now, a
few other boys were also listening to the teacher's explanation
with interest. Bobaji then explained to the young lads how
Muslims and Hindus have co-existed in harmony in Kashmir
for centuries.

He told them about the spirit of Kashmiriyat and how
the festivals of Hinduism and Islam are celebrated by people
of both religions. Kashmiriyat is the centuries-old indigenous
tradition of communal harmony and religious syncretism in
the Kashmir Valley. It exemplifies the joint Hindu–Muslim
culture, festivals, language, cuisine and clothing in the Kashmir
Valley. In the spirit of Kashmiriyat, festivals of Hinduism and
Islam are celebrated by both faiths. It was started by Sultan
Zain-ul-Abidin in the sixteenth century, who promoted a
policy of religious tolerance. He banned the slaughter of cows
to be sensitive to Hindus. He allowed the Hindus to build
their temples and follow the personal law according to the
Dharmashastras. Nazir's young mind could not follow all of
it, but he grasped the spirit of it. What he particularly found
fascinating was the story of the Kashmiri mystic Lal Ded, in
which her body turned into a mound of flowers, half of which
was cremated by the Hindus and the other half buried by
Muslims and serves as an emblem of the Kashmiriyat that
keeps it alive until today. As per another account, her body
turned into liquid in a basin, which was cremated and buried
by Hindus and Muslims, respectively, as she was revered by
both faiths.[6]

The second memory, again from his childhood, was from
the time he was travelling to another village in the higher

---

[6] 'Kashmir Shaivism', n.d., https://shaivism.net/kashmirigems/lalded1.html.

reaches with a friend and his family to visit a distant cousin. En route, they saw a few foreign men and women walking with backpacks. They were laughing, chatting and taking pictures with their cameras. He asked his friend about them. His friend's father explained to both of them, 'They are foreign tourists who have come for trekking in Kashmir.'

'Why would they want to walk when they have the money to travel by bus?' Nazir wanted to know.

'Because our Kashmir is so beautiful, they don't want the journey to end so soon.'

The third such incident had to do with a retired soldier in the village. Sometimes, he would recount tales from his army days to a few young boys. His descriptions of army life and soldierly activities always made for a fascinating evening for Nazir and others who sat around and listened. One day, Nazir asked him, '*Aapne bandook chalai hai* [Have you ever fired a gun]?' The soldier replied with pride in his voice: '*Maine teen jung mein ladai ladi hai* [I've fought in three wars].' Nazir was impressed, and his young mind concluded that it must be a heroic thing to be at war. He suddenly said, 'I will also fight wars when I grow up.' The retired *fauji* (soldier) laughed as he said, 'Oh, you are very brave.' Little did he know that this young boy would one day become the recipient of the highest medal for bravery.

During these days, he also heard other men in his village talk in whispers about the jihad being waged by young men and the atrocities being committed by the police and the army.

This was very confusing because he was torn between two thoughts—which side to pick when he grew up?

But schooling could not last because the family's financial troubles were growing. As the eldest son, Nazir had to leave school and share the family's responsibilities. He started working in a carpet factory when he was barely ten years old. His area was known for traditional carpets locally called *kaleen*, and almost every home was involved in the craft. Every street corner also had a small factory.

Carpet weaving was not easy. Sometimes the threads would get entangled in the old looms, and sometimes they would break. But this young lad, who worked on old looms, was assiduous. Being exposed to such hardships so early in life made Nazir wise and mature far beyond his years. Once he learned the basic craft in a few months at the factory, he decided to make carpets at home so that he could teach his younger brothers and expand the income base. His dreams about studying at a school seemed to be firmly over.

In the 1990s, things started changing. Strange men started moving in the shadows in the village. They would sometimes be seen talking to the youth or visiting the mosques during Friday prayers. Unlike the retired army soldier who would brag about his exploits in the village centre in a loud voice, the strangers spoke in whispers and always restricted themselves to the dark corners of someone's home. One day, Nazir and his brothers heard gunshots. They were scared, but also intrigued. Their father, however, forbade them from going outside.

With the exodus of Kashmiri Pandits in 1990, many things changed. Though Nazir did not see such departures in his village, as there were no Hindus in Cheki Ashmuji, he heard about them from others.

One evening, Aslam (name changed), an older friend who had worked with him in the factory, said there was a meeting in the village and persuaded Nazir to come along. Nazir and two of his factory friends went to listen to the town leader.

Fifty to sixty men had already gathered under a big tree. Some were seated on a few chairs facing the crowd. Others stood around or squatted. Nazir and his friends climbed up a mound around two trees, which were a little away, but from this height they could see and hear everything. A man with a red beard, whom Nazir did not recognize, was speaking in an agitated manner. 'The Pandits have suppressed us for centuries. They say we are brothers but give us step-brotherly treatment. They take the cream and give us skimmed milk. They must go.' A couple of elders argued against it, saying that we have lived together in harmony for generations. We have participated in each other's families and festivals. That is the strength of Kashmiriyat. This syncretism is unique in the world. If Pandits leave Kashmir, then there will be no Kashmiriyat. Several younger men started raising slogans like, 'Pandits take advantage of us because of such sentimental fools.' Someone shouted, 'Is this the way to talk to elders?' It was getting noisy, and the young lads climbed down from their perch and slipped away unnoticed.

The Kashmiri Pandits had been a favoured section of the population of the Valley during the Hindu Dogra rule. While a significant percentage of them started leaving the Valley as a consequence of the 1950 land reforms, they began to leave in much greater numbers in the 1990s during the eruption of militancy, following persecution and threats by radical Islamists and militants. The events of 19 January 1990 were particularly vicious. On that day, mosques issued declarations that the Kashmiri Pandits were kafirs and that the males would either have to leave Kashmir, convert to Islam or be killed.[7] The Kashmiri Muslims were instructed to identify Pandit homes so they could be systematically targeted for conversion or killing. One has heard of many such tales.[8]

A later report by the J&K government explained the situation more precisely: between 1989 and 2004, as many as 219 people from this community were killed, and an

---

[7] Wikipedia contributors, 'Kashmiri Pandits', Wikipedia, October 2, 2023, https://en.wikipedia.org/wiki/Kashmiri_Pandit#Exodus_from_Kashmir_.281985.E2.80.931995.29%20A.

[8] PTI, 'Kashmiri Pandits Observed January 19 as "Holocaust Day"', Print, 19 January 2022, https://theprint.in/india/kashmiri-pandits-observed-january-19-as-holocaust-day/807813/.

exodus of over 1,50,000 of the total Pandit population of approximately 2,00,000 took place. The condition of many of the refugee camps for Kashmiri Pandits in Jammu was dismal.

One day, Aslam asked Nazir to accompany him to a nearby village to deliver a letter. Nazir was reluctant because his father was not at home, and there was something strange about the way Aslam was behaving. When Aslam insisted, Nazir told his Ammi (mother) he would be back soon and left with his friend. When they reached the village, Aslam pulled out a bulky envelope from the waistband of his trousers. He went inside, while Nazir waited outside. On their way back, when Nazir pressed him for details, Aslam simply said, 'I am only helping out someone who is helping us all.' The tone of his voice did not encourage more questions, so Nazir left it at that. But that night, he kept wondering what it could be. Was Aslam involved in something wrong? Was he helping terrorists?

Nazir was getting better at carpet weaving. Two of his brothers had also started picking up the skills. In time, they would be able to supplement the family's income. Nazir told his mother, 'Ammi, one day, we brothers will make you proud by making you a kaleen.' His mother's eyes grew moist as she said, 'You all are working at such a young age when you should be studying in school,' and hugged them all. Nazir too felt overwhelmed.

One evening, while he was returning home, two older boys came along with an unknown man and needlessly began taunting Nazir. They went out of their way to pick a fight. Nazir lashed out when one of them abused his Abbu (father). They were all older, and it was three against one. Nazir could not do much as one held him and the other punched him in the stomach before warning him to keep quiet about them. Nazir was more bewildered than hurt.

Such incidents started occurring more frequently. After a few days, Aslam came home to say someone wanted to meet him. Nazir replied that he was not interested, and he if did go, it would only be after informing Abba. Aslam quickly responded, 'Meri maan [listen to me], don't tell your Abba, and don't tell anyone else.'

A few days later, Aslam came over to his house and asked him to come for a walk. Since Nazir had not seen him for some days, he was happy to oblige. He liked talking to his friend to make sense of many things that puzzled him, particularly about unknown young men who were often seen in the village. They were tall, well-built and mostly bearded. Some of them looked dangerous. One of them was also seen with the two older boys who had picked a fight with him.

Aslam later said he could sense that things were changing. The strangers said they were relatives of some people in the village, or perhaps they were not. It was better not to annoy them. Aslam told Nazir: 'If you do what I say and help in carrying a message or a package or running some such errand, no one will mess with you.' 'Why?' Nazir wanted to know. 'Once it is known you are helping the cause, no one will want to mess with you.' Aslam reassured Nazir that no one would trouble him or his family. 'We are young men now. We have given up school and are helping our parents. It is also our duty to see that no harm comes to our families.' To this, Nazir had no answer. He was obviously in agreement with this part.

Nazir agreed to accompany Aslam the next time he went on an errand. Young boys were preferred to run errands or carry packages, as neither the police nor the 'agencies' (euphemism for intelligence agencies or their 'sources') would suspect these youngsters. Nazir was asked a lot of questions by the two unknown, bearded men when he finally met them. They spoke in a firm but unthreatening voice. It was more like an interview, where they established that Nazir came from a poor family with good values. He was contributing to the family's income and had three younger brothers.

He was a bit confused about the environment of mistrust in the village. He could not be blamed for that; his entire generation was confused, as strong attempts were being made to claim the minds of the children. Finding some reassurance, he agreed to help run errands for these men and their group in return for some financing and a feeling of security. Thus, he became an overground worker (OGW) for the al-Jihad group. In the tenuous and volatile setting of Kashmir in the early 1990s, a young boy from a weaker section of society looked for reassurance that he belonged. In time, they would judge the resilience and strength of these boys, see for themselves how they held out when the chips were down and after a suitable time period had elapsed, they would select some of them for initiation and training into militant activities. Some of them would eventually be sent to Pakistan for training in terrorist camps.

Training in these terrorist camps included physical conditioning, weapon training, field craft, navigation and above all, ideological retraining—infusing the young minds with the idea of jihad. In these camps, they met and trained with young boys belonging to Pakistan-Occupied Kashmir (POK) or the rest of Pakistan as well. After the training was over, these boys were infiltrated into J&K for an agreed duration, and their families were promised or given an agreed sum of money. After reporting to a local terror module in J&K, these foreign terrorists (FTs, as they are referred to in the army) had to carry out some acts of violence to earn that money. After all, the handlers also got funding from other Islamist organizations that supported terror around the globe. I particularly call them Islamists and not Islamic, for obvious reasons.

It was a full-blown cottage industry.

Chapter 3

Unrest in Heaven: The Turbulent 1990s

In 1993, I was posted to Kargil as the Brigade Major. Those two years were truly valuable for understanding the state much more deeply. This was essential because J&K was more than just Jammu and Kashmir. Ladakh is very unique in many ways. It is a high-altitude desert that remains cut off for half the year due to heavy snowfall. While the Kargil War between India and Pakistan in 1999 and, more recently, the India–China standoff in eastern Ladakh, have increased national awareness about this remote area, during my time it was a lesser-known land, full of mystique and home to some interesting historical facts. Kargil is roughly midway between Srinagar and Leh. One had to interact constantly with 15 Corps HQ in Srinagar and Division HQ at Leh. As a major in the army, it gave me wide exposure to two extremes, but one that would stand me in good stead in my later days as well.

This is the land where Alexander's army was stopped by the mighty Indus, forcing them to retreat. Some soldiers or stragglers stayed back on the banks of the Indus River in these mountains. They remained reclusive, inhabiting the four villages of Darchik, Dah, Garkhun and Hanuthang. The inhabitants call themselves a pure Aryan race. Several researchers from the western world, mainly Germany, have come here to study their antecedents. There was also an apocryphal story that, in the early 1990s, a couple of German women tourists travelled to these villages with the intention of impregnating themselves with 'pure' Aryan genes.

The demography of Kargil District is predominantly Shia. The population is sparse, and people here do not largely identify with the grievances of Kashmiris, who are mostly Sunni. In fact, they come from the same stock as the people

of Gilgit-Baltistan, in POK. The moral and financial support
from Iran is strong and is channelled through an active
Khomeini Memorial Trust in Kargil.

Heavy snowfall cuts off all Ladakh for six months each
year. Zoji La Pass from Srinagar and Rohtang Pass on the
Himachal flank, being on the Greater Himalayan Range,
get buried under snow. Supplies for the winter months,
from rations to fuel to medicines to LPG cylinders to Maggi
noodles and everything in between, have to be stocked
up during the summer months. It is called advance winter
stocking. Nowadays, the passes close for shorter durations
because of better snow clearance equipment, and tunnels are
being constructed under these passes. But in those days, we
used to remain cut off for six months.

Despite these disruptions, it was always astounding to learn
that thousands of tonnes of cargo were moved through one
single road, which was used by both civilians and the military.
As Brigade Major, I did not deal with this logistic nightmare
directly, but came into contact with the operational realm of
road opening—soldiers physically searching the road inch by
inch for explosives planted by terrorists every day. This was the
fallout of the anti-terrorist operations in the Kashmir Valley. If
maintaining movement during those days was a challenge, one
can imagine what a nightmare it must be today since the force
levels have been upgraded to a corps, more so after China's
adventurism in eastern Ladakh in the summer of 2020.

It was during this time, in November 1993, that the siege
of Hazratbal mosque took place. Approximately eighteen to
twenty terrorists had taken over the holy shrine. Hazratbal
mosque is a very sacred place because it claims to host a holy
relic—a hair of Prophet Mohammed.

The militants had taken refuge in the shrine when the
army cordoned off the area for a search operation. The
army laid siege to the shrine, which continued for more than
a month. Life was disrupted in Kashmir, and around fifty

people were killed, almost forty of them on 22 October at Bijbehara, Anantnag, during a protest when a mob turned violent after Friday prayers. They began marching through the streets, shouting pro-independence slogans and demanding an end to the Hazratbal siege. They clashed with the Border Security Force (BSF), which was trying to bring the situation under control.

Towards the end of the Hazratbal operation, there was significant coordination as well as grave misunderstandings between different agencies and forces. the complex dynamics of the administration and different security forces, including the intelligence agencies. It was really tough for the forces to operate, although to their credit, they did a fine job of it, under the circumstances.

The Hazratbal stand-off was finally brought to an end after intense negotiations with the help of local Muslim clergymen, family members and some politicians who had goodwill with the terrorist network. Under the deal struck between the authorities and the militants on 16 November 1993, the authorities gave the militants safe passage inside the shrine.

While the Valley was undergoing problems in the densely inhabited areas, my responsibilities were on the border. My life revolved around a routine exchange of fire on the LoC. But situations would develop suddenly. We got word that a group of twenty-eight terrorists attempted to infiltrate through the Mashkoh Valley in Dras, which is the second-coldest inhabited place on earth after Siberia. It was after several years that militants were attempting to infiltrate into the Valley through this route of higher reaches. The militants had a major disadvantage: the local population did not identify with the Kashmiri cause, denying them a local support base. They also met with another formidable obstacle: a Gorkha battalion deployed on their infiltration route. The operations lasted two days, as the militants had hidden in a couple of caves. Sadly, we lost two soldiers, but all twenty-eight terrorists were eliminated. Once the operation was over, I was puzzled and moved by what must have driven these young men to undertake such a venture—they were wearing normal sneakers, which had caused their feet to become misshapen due to long exposure to heavy snow. In contrast, several years later, one noticed that the terrorists wore very sophisticated snow clothing and boots while negotiating snow-covered areas.

I spoke often with the JAKLI jawans of my regiment, and what they conveyed was that the situation was grim in their villages and turning worse by the day. During January 1994, I was enjoying thick snow and even practising skiing on improvised ski slopes near the Kargil helipad when preparations for the Republic Day parade were underway in Srinagar. Intensive operations were being conducted against the disruption of the parade and the flag-hosting ceremony by the militants. Despite all these security precautions, the militants struck when the Governor was delivering his customary address in Jammu. Three bombs went off in quick succession. Fortunately, the Governor was unhurt, but the casualties were heavy: twelve dead and over fifty injured in the blasts and the subsequent melee.

It was clear that the authorities needed to do something to stop the slide in its tracks. One heard of many initiatives, but in early 1994, there were trickles of news through the informal grapevine that a contra rebel group called Ikhwan was being raised. Several terrorists, mostly from the Jammu and Kashmir Student Liberation Front (JKSLF), a pro-independence group, had been persuaded to join the army's efforts to eradicate terrorism. I also learned it was working well at most places, as these surrendered militants could generate real-time intelligence on the terrorists' movements. Their participation in operations also added huge value, as they knew the terrorists' modus operandi well. In fact, they sometimes even knew some of the terrorists being targeted.

The terrorist groups had their own fault lines. There was a strong undercurrent of tension between the pro-independence and pro-Pakistan groups. The former wanted an independent Kashmir, while pro-Pakistan groups like HM stood for merging Kashmir with Pakistan, which was in line with the agenda of Pakistan. In June 1994, a highly respected religious leader, Qazi Nissar Ahmed was assassinated, leading to strong protests. The reaction to the assassination also indicated that a significant segment of the population was moderate and tired of the terrorists' role in disturbing peace in the Valley.

In March 1995, a group of militants—many of whom were foreigners—led by Mast Gul took control of the fourteenth-century Charar-i-Sharief shrine in the Budgam hill town, 28 km from Srinagar. Mast Gul was the nom de guerre of Haroon Khan, Pakistan's Afghan-hardened fighter. The *mazaar*, or shrine, has been the resting place of the saint, Sheikh Noor-ud-Din Noorani (RA), since 1438. Born Nund Rishi in 1377, the saint pioneered *rishiat*[9] in Kashmir and became popular as Alamdar-e-Kashmir, or the flag-bearer of Kashmir. He is hailed as one of the pioneers of Kashmiriyat, something dear to my JAKLI regiment and an integral part of its ethos.

The siege lasted two months. The shrine was ultimately destroyed in a fire that began after the militants holed up inside triggered the blasts and attacked the BSF personnel. Twenty militants, two soldiers and five civilians were killed in the confrontation, but the public was informed that Mast Gul and several of his associates escaped. Later, speaking at the Idea Exchange programme organized by the *Indian Express*

---

[9] Rishiat or Sufism was the syncretic concept started by Nund Rishi or Sheikh ul Alam in which both Hindus and Muslims worshipped the same sages.

in July 2012, former defence minister Jaswant Singh stated that he knew 'for a fact that Mast Gul vacated the dargah, and he was escorted all the way to the LoC and permitted to go'. When Mast Gul returned to Pakistan, he was given a hero's welcome by the Jamaat-e-Islami,[10] which showcased him at several meetings.

Sitting far away from Srinagar, one could discern that there were so many wheels within wheels playing out—various groups with different interests. Even versions of the same event would be vastly different. While the terrorist groups had their divisions, the situation with the authorities was no less complex. Or ugly. For a military man like me trained in the value of the unitary chain of command, the confusion at the highest levels due to distributed responsibility and a lack of accountability was ungainly. The security forces in the Valley were serving under a complex dynamic, which was no doubt necessitated by the times and context.

For the first time Rajesh Pilot had been appointed as the interior minister, and S.B. Chavan was the home minister. I could never fathom the tricky balancing act the army authorities needed to play to adjust to the dynamics between the Governor during Governor's Rule in the state and the ministry from Delhi.

Gen. K.V. Krishna Rao, the governor, was a retired army chief who had as his advisor the retired Corps Commander of the Srinagar-based 15 Corps, Lt Gen. M.A. Zaki. These are truly important decision-making positions whose significance I realized two decades later when I was the Corps Commander in Srinagar and the ex-officio security advisor to the Governor and the chief minister. Several

---

[10] IE Online, 'Charar-e-Sharief Militant Mast Gul Resurfaces with Pakistani Taliban', *Indian Express*, February 6, 2014, https://indianexpress.com/article/india/india-others/charar-e-sharief-militant-mast-gul-resurfaces-with-pakistani-taliban-2/.

senior officers travelling between Srinagar and Leh would have to have a night halt in Kargil. It was unusual for a major to get such opportunities, but as a Brigade Major, I got to interact with them. The situation in the Valley was the favourite topic of discussion because, by then, it had become clear that, contrary to earlier beliefs, this militancy was not a passing law and order problem.

While the state and the security forces led by the army were trying to contain the violence, the political landscape was abuzz. A conglomeration of several outfits combined to set up the All Parties Hurriyat Conference (APHC) in 1993. It would be a political forum for the separatists' movement, and Mirwaiz Umar Farooq would be its chairman. He was barely twenty years old and had been propelled into the leadership of the J&K Awami Action Committee after the assassination of his father, Mirwaiz Farooq. However, a much older Syed Ali Shah Geelani was the better-known face of the separatists and presided over the agitation for several terms. The constituents of the APHC, however, were not homogeneous: some were pro-independence while others preferred merger with Pakistan. It also had strong links with terrorist organizations. Over the years, the role of the Hurriyat in the political landscape waxed and waned, as did its effective control over the militant factions and the violent youth. It was fraught with internecine factionalism as it engaged with the governments in India and Pakistan. They also differed on engaging with terrorist tanzeems.

Chapter 4

Thorn on a Thorn: The Birth of Ikhwan

A Bold Experiment

In 1988, there was an influx of Kashmiri youth to Pakistan for arms training. The main insurgent group behind all this was the Jammu and Kashmir Liberation Front (JKLF), headed by Ashfaq Majeed Wani. The other prominent leaders of the JKLF during that period were Mohammed Yasin Malik, Sheikh Hamid, Hilal Ahmed Beg, Javid Ahmed Mir and Ajaz Ahmed Dar. Most of them were from poor families and the leaders incited and motivated them with a heady mixture of money, religion and machismo to wage jihad against government forces and join the fight for the liberation of Kashmir.

With Pakistan finding this development an easy and cheap way to create trouble for India, the terrorist organizations grew rapidly in numbers. And they also rapidly multiplied. By 1990, this competition among these organizations led to two developments: the mass exodus of the Kashmiri Pandits and a tussle among the groups.

The constant infighting among the groups led to one of the leaders, Hilal Ahmed, Beg splitting away from the JKLF and starting the Jammu and Kashmir Student Liberation Front (JKSLF). As the name implies, the majority of JKSLF comprised educated youth. The JKSLF, too, started sending educated youths to Pakistan. Both the JKLF and the JKSLF were more popular than others in Kashmir because both were pro-*azadi*: independence for Kashmir. While Pakistan was providing financial and material support to these groups, it was inwardly not pleased with their inclination for

35

independence, as Pakistan was gunning for the assimilation of Kashmir into Pakistan.

Soon, Pakistan had a change of strategy. It wanted all militant groups to be pro-Pakistan, and the ones not cooperating would be denied funds, training and launch pads. The JKLF and the JKSLF bore the direct brunt of the decision. Pakistan also wanted the two groups to sign an Instrument of Accession with them, which they refused, having set their sights on independence. One former militant leader, code-named Romeo, explained to me later how it felt to be denied support. He said it was very frustrating to be staying in the training camps awaiting orders to infiltrate, which were not forthcoming. They were also not free to leave the camps. It was a Catch-22 situation between not enjoying their stay in Pakistan and not being able to return to their families in India.

With the two major terror groups not falling in line, Pakistan began creating new militant outfits, namely the Hizbul Mujahideen (HM), the Muslim Janbaaz Force (MJF), the Al Umar Mujahideen (AUM), the Tehreeq-ul-Mujahideen (TUM), Allah Tigers, al-Jihad, Al Badr (all pro-Pakistan) and several other smaller groups. Pakistan ensured that all the new groups were supportive of a merger with Pakistan, and most were forced to sign the Instrument of Accession.

In 1994, United Jehad Council (literally, network of fighters) was formed in POK at the behest of the Inter-Services Intelligence (ISI) to coordinate the activities of all terrorist groups. It was obviously led by the HM.

After a while, the JKSLF started feeling the consequences of the cessation of support from Pakistan. With his constituents feeling restive, Hilal Ahmed Beg approached Pakistan to remedy the situation and later even signed the memorandum of understanding to be a pro-Pakistan group. It was, however, not a consensual decision within the JKSLF.

Since it consisted of educated youth who were much better informed than most other organizations, internal dissensions soon resulted in a split led by Hilal Ahmed Beg, which gave rise to the Ikhwan-ul-Muslimeen (IUM).

The IUM grew rapidly, and the members were reorganized to provide a major role for the youth of Anantnag, who were the most educated and most numerous in the group. Sajaad Ahmed Kanue was made District Commander in Anantnag. In one of the early decisions, Kanue sent a batch of motivated and educated youths from Anantnag (persons such as Shiekh Tahir, Shoukat Ahmed Bhat and Gulzar Ahmed Kanue, who would become better known later) to Pakistan for arms training.

With the militancy getting further entrenched, the militants' idealism was also giving way to a struggle for dominance, a tussle for influence, even petty crime in the name of militancy. The IUM group soon returned from the training camp in POK but was increasingly disillusioned to see a drastic change in the attitudes and ideologies of various militant groups in the Valley. The groups were fighting less with the security forces and more with each other to gain an upper hand over one another. It was inevitable that the IUM also got involved in inter-group rivalry in order to safeguard their interests.

In 1993, matters started taking a vicious turn. The HM, under the leadership of Mohammed Ahsan Dar, Mohammed Ashraf Sunnu and Shamsul Haq, wanted to exist as the sole militant organization in Kashmir and wanted all the other groups to merge with them. To achieve this objective, it began targeting groups such as the JKLF, al-Jihad, TUM, AUM, MJF and the JKSLF. The clashes resulted in the elimination of many educated young men from other militant organizations whose ideology was to gain independence. Whoever dared to challenge the HM's ideology was either eliminated, disarmed or tortured. By 1994, the HM had almost finished JKLF, which was very popular with the general populace by virtue of being pro-independence and their humane connection with local people. Soon, the HM emerged as the most dreaded and powerful group among the militants.

The IUM too felt the wrath of the HM, and most of their cadres were eliminated or disarmed. The Supreme Commander of the IUM, Hilal Beg, reshuffled the command structure of the group, made Sajaad Ahmed Kanue Deputy Supreme Commander, and shifted him to Srinagar from Anantnag. Since IUM comprised educated youths, they could not reconcile getting caught in the middle between the security forces and HM. Many were either killed in inter-group rivalry or deserted the organization and this resulted in disillusionment among the IUM cadres.

The inter-group rivalry was at its peak during this period, and IUM had to make many structural adjustments to face the pressure. Sheikh Tahir, Liyaqat Ali Khan and Shabir Baduri were made heads of the cadres in South Kashmir while the North Kashmir IUM was headed by Mohammad Yusuf Parray, better known as Kuka Parrey alias Jamshid Sherazi.

Of course, all these developments were being closely watched by the army, J&K Police and intelligence agencies. It was only natural that the Army assisted by intelligence agencies, took the initiative and started making contact with IUM cadres as well as leaders, particularly Shiekh Tahir and Kuka Parrey. The objective was to motivate them to collaborate with the army and assist in combating militancy and bloodshed.

The initial overtures showed good signs of success. Encouraged, a more ambitious thought process was set in motion. It was decided to get these terrorists to surrender and assimilate them in the state's effort to neutralize other terror groups.

Contra rebels are not a new phenomenon. It has been tried in several parts of the world in more complex forms.

During the early phase of the Cold War, it was a strategy used by an outside agency to fund disgruntled citizens in a dictatorship to form a militia, such as the one the US created in Cuba to fight Fidel Castro. The most controversial was the Iran–Contra Affair, which became a scandal because the CIA was secretly selling arms to Iran, whose Khomeini regime was under sanctions, and the proceeds were used to bankroll rebels in Nicaragua, called Contras.[11] The chief strategy was what Col Oliver North of the National Security Council described as 'plausible deniability' of an illegal and clandestine operation. In India, there was nothing clandestine about Ikhwan.

It was increasingly positioned as an important part of an overt counter-terrorism strategy, and by the end of it, would even be formalized as a part of the military. However, when the Chhattisgarh government tried something similar called Salwa Judum (peace march in Gondi language) with tribal youth to fight Naxalites or Marxist-Leninists in the state, the Supreme Court shut it down in 2011, terming it illegal and unconstitutional.

In Kashmir, it was a bold experiment to correct a fast-deteriorating law and order situation. The paradigm of using surrendered militants officially was Rajesh Pilot's brainchild since he was the union minister of state for internal security, a ministry specially created for tackling the situation in J&K. The groups involved were heavily armed, and another country with a contiguous border was involved by proxy in supporting them.

Once it began, the IUM cadres surrendered in larger numbers and joined hands with the army to fight militancy. The cadres restructured the IUM Supreme Council with the selection of the new commanders, interestingly, through a

---

[11] Wikipedia contributors, 'Iran–Contra Affair - Wikipedia', November 7, 2023, https://en.wikipedia.org/wiki/Iran%E2%80%93Contra_affair.

draw of lots. The new order had Liaqat Ali Khan as chairman of the IUM, Sheikh Tahir as Operational Commander of South Kashmir, and Kuka Parrey as chairman of the North Kashmir unit.

The name of the organization was also changed from IUM to Ikhwan (meaning 'brothers' in Arabic). Historically, the Ikhwan was the first Saudi army made up of traditionally nomadic tribesmen whose clerics or teachers were dedicated to the idea of the purification and unification of Islam. Besides IUM, there was another group operated by Javed Ahmad Shah, who had been working with the J&K Police's Special Operations Group to counter other militants. They were all merged together under the overall umbrella of **Ikhwan**.

Once the group became a working reality, it provided many advantages. Chief among them was our ability to better understand the psychographics of a terrorist. I spoke to some of them regarding their terrorist training camps. These members, mostly young boys, were clandestinely taken to POK and beyond. Trackers who knew the terrain well and who knew where deployment gaps were on the long LoC guided them across it.

Once there, they were shifted to training camps in POK or taken beyond to Jalalabad or Khost in Afghanistan. One of them told me that they were made to work as porters for the first one month, but the training camps were run on military lines with a disciplined training routine. They were put through physical training and toughening, firing, navigation, explosives and improvised explosive device (IED) training. Then there was always the ideological brainwashing. This included a range of talks ranging from Hindu (kafir) domination to denial of rightful opportunities to Muslims to invoking the Holy Quran to justify the jihad against the kafir, hence against India. The focus was on the latter, with the lure of *jannat* (heaven) and seventy-two *hoors* (celestial angels). The training camps were similar, whether they were in Afghanistan or POK.

Even as the collaboration between the Ikhwan and army stabilized, there were rumblings of discontent. Sajaad Kanue, the Deputy Supreme Commander of IUM, tried to motivate Ikhwan cadres to rejoin the militancy, which resulted in Shabir Baduri returning to the terrorists' fold. However, Sheikh Tahir and Liyaqat Ali Khan remained steadfast, continued to operate with the army and kept the existence of Ikhwan alive.

The Ikhwan were reorganized and trained to fight against militancy. An Ikhwan training camp was established under the aegis of Rashtriya Rifles, wherein they were trained in their endeavour for peace and to eliminate terrorism from its roots. The training imparted to Ikhwan gave them a sense of discipline and reassurance. Subsequently, the role of Ikhwan cadres was felt in almost all successful counter-terrorist operations in the Valley. When successful operations brought long-lost peace and tranquility to the state, the general public, tired of living in such disturbed conditions, started supporting the Ikhwan. Seeing the groundswell of support, even a splinter group of HM joined the Ikhwan.

But the life of an Ikhwan was not easy. It was tricky because they and their families were in constant danger from the militants. The Ikhwan cadres lived in their homes or in groups in their villages and were allowed to keep their weapons with them. They maintained close contact with the army, or the RR companies deployed nearby. While it worked well for the army and the police for the purpose for which it was created, allowing ex-militants to live among the population with weapons had its own pitfalls and excesses, which will be discussed later.

By keeping an ear to the ground, they were able to generate actionable real-time intelligence—inputs that were current and actionable. Many operations could be launched with great success. The Ikhwan leaders later recalled with respect the bravery of Sub Abdul Qayoom Itoo, who operated fearlessly with teams of PARA COMMANDOS, which neutralized over eighty terrorists.

With each success under this arrangement, other terrorist groups and their supporters saw the Ikhwan as traitors. Since the Ikhwan cadres were living in their homes and not in the security of an army camp, they were extremely vulnerable. Two measures were, therefore, taken. First, the Ikhwans were helped to shift their base often so they would not stay at the same place for long. And second, Ikhwan camps were created to give them a secure place to stay and operate from. I have been to Nazir Wani's house in Kulgam, in one such residential area.

While the military aspect was primary, the security forces understood that normalcy would return only in a peaceful social setting. The Ikhwan was supported by the army to carry out social work for the benefit of the local populace.

The then Supreme Commander of the Ikhwan, Sheikh Tahir in South Kashmir and Kuka Parray in North Kashmir, were enthusiastic about the project, to make connections with the local populations, while in the central areas of Pulwama and Budgam, the Ikhwan project was replicated with support from the Central Reserve Police Force (CRPF), the Border Security Force (BSF) and the police.

By 1996, the Ikhwan had managed to assist in neutralizing a large number of terrorists. Neutralizing would mean either elimination in operations or getting the militants to surrender. Neither was an easy task. While the role of Ikhwan will remain controversial, over time they made a significant contribution to bringing the situation so much under control that the government could contemplate holding elections in the state after a gap of nearly a decade.

The National Conference, which was the only regional party to contest the election, won fifty-seven seats in 1996, and Farooq Abdullah became chief minister. A.S. Dulat, former head of the Research and Analysis Wing (R&AW) writes in his book *Kashmir: The Vajpayee Years*: 'The 1996 election was a masterstroke because it revived the political process and broke the back of militancy.'

Ironically, however, its success may have been good for the state, but it was not necessarily good for the Ikhwan itself. While the concept of using the militants to take out other militants was brilliant, it was construed as an ad hoc solution. To an extent, this was understandable because the person designing it needed to be careful if something were to go wrong.

Some of the cadres started to indulge in extortion. When some cadres of the Ikhwan indulged in the brutal killing of terrorists in public, other groups would soon start to use their name to exploit the situation. Some even started illegally felling trees to make money through the timber trade. As a result, the Ikhwan started earning a bad name.

The tallest Ikhwan leader, Kuka Parray, won an election and was elected to the Legislative Assembly. When Parray got busy with his MLA duties, some parts of Ikhwan got politicized and other parts were neglected. This led to excesses and wayward behaviour by some of them, giving a bad name to the concept of the Ikhwan.

Somewhere around the turn of the century, the Ikhwan, as an independent entity with no defined terms of reference, started to lose steam. After the elections of 2002, it was decided to close down the Ikhwan and raise a TA battalion of the JAKLI—Home and Hearth (H&H) comprising those surrendered terrorists who were willing to join.

Chapter 5

Nazir the Ikhwan

Nazir joined Ikhwan in December 1995 and up to 2003, worked with a Rashtriya Rifles Battalion (RR Bn) along with Lance Naik Zahoor Ahmad, Lance Naik Mushtaq Ahmad Mir (also known as Maulvi because of his fastidious religious habits), Mohammed Amin Dar and Jahangir Ahmad Wani (who left after initial training with the Territorial Army Battalion [TA Bn]). These men formed bonds of friendship that were thicker than blood. When you share life-threatening experiences on a daily basis together, you learn to depend on each other, and you trust each other with your lives. There is no bond stronger than that.

Nazir and his young friends initially ran errands, passed messages, guided the soldiers to known and unknown locations and acted as interpreters. Their advantage was that no one suspected these young boys. Slowly, they graduated to more substantive contributions to the collective effort. The Ikhwan had to lead risky lives, which held risks for their families as well.

The Ikhwan cadres lived in their homes or in groups in their villages and were allowed to keep their weapons with them. They kept in close contact with the army or RR companies deployed nearby. By keeping an ear to the ground, they were able to generate real-time intelligence.

Purveying actionable intelligence, combined with their knowledge of the terrorist mind, made Ikhwan very effective. Soon, terrorist groups were truly fed up with the Ikhwan and targeted the cadres. When the perceived risk became high, the government set up Ikhwan camps that were fully secured in many parts of the state. Nazir lived in an Ikhwan camp in Kulgam.

Nazir got married in 1998, and his wife Mahajabeen came to live with him in the Ikhwan camp. The families were not happy about his arrangement since they wanted her to live with the in-laws as is customary. Nazir, however, insisted that this way they would all be secure, especially when the men went out for operations. This also gave them an opportunity to lead a normal family life.

On 3 April 2001, Nazir was at the Kulgam Ikhwan camp with Mahajabeen. Upon hearing a knock at the door, he asked Mahajabeen to go inside and open the door. An agitated Mushtaq, aka Maulvi, informed Nazir that a couple of Afghani terrorists had been spotted in Mohammad Pora village. 'We will go ahead and establish a surveillance base to guide the soldiers when they arrive.'

Nazir reached out for his ammunition pouches, which were hanging on the wall, and got ready with enthusiasm. Mahajabeen watched his every move while he got ready and put on his shoes with trepidation, careful not to say anything. This happened every time he went for an operation. Who knows what may happen? Wives always have this unsaid fear. Watching her tense countenance, Nazir reassured her, '*Mujhe kuchh nahin hoga. Fikr mat karo* [Nothing will happen to me. Don't worry].' Easier said than done. But what else could he do? Or say? Paradoxically, the same applied to her as well.

They took a little longer than usual to reach Mohammad Pora, as they were moving cautiously, trying to avoid populated areas. One could never be sure where their informers would be lurking. It happened so many times that informers in nearby villages would alert the terrorists in advance, which helped them escape before the army reached the spot. In April, the rest of India was turning warm, but not Kashmir. The mountains were still covered with snow, and the air was still cold. Were it not for an operation, it would have been a lovely day for the kind of foreign tourists he had seen during his childhood.

In Mohammad Pora, a soldier behind him tapped Nazir on the shoulder and pointed at the cluster of three houses. 'I think we should stop and fan out now,' said the Company Commander. He accompanied the Company Commander as he checked the cordon. They were moving cautiously, crawling most of the time, taking shelter in the trees, bushes, brick walls or anything else they could find. Funnily enough, sometimes even cattle offered cover in innovative ways. It was critical to maintain surprise, at least until the cordon was fully established. If the terrorists were alerted early, they could escape through the gaps in the cordon. Soldiers making up the cordon were nearly in place when a burst of automatic firing broke the silence. They ducked to the ground reflexively. Such reflexive action is a part of training and has been a lifesaver many times.

Nazir started crawling towards the spot where he had left Mushtaq and others. As he crossed a couple of soldiers behind a bund, he saw they were firing bursts of bullets from their light machine guns. But no target was clearly visible. He cautioned them not to waste ammunition until they had a clear line of sight at the target.

The cluster of three houses had been surrounded. Sometimes the buildings merged into one another. Now that the soldiers with light machine guns (LMGs) were not firing indiscriminately, the exchange of fire was sporadic. As he was nearing the spot where he left his buddies, a movement caught his eye in the overgrown shrubbery not very far from him. Someone else had seen it too. Because a couple of shots were fired at the movement from a depression a few metres from him. He crawled towards them. Just then, there was a brief but intense exchange of automatic bursts of rifle fire from both sides. His buddies were in a slushy nala, a ditch. As he crawled in after making himself known, a soldier whispered rather loudly, 'Mushtaq ko goli lagi [Mushtaq has been shot].' That spurred Nazir. With an adrenaline rush, unmindful of the slush, he crawled up to his friend, held his hand to reassure him, and pulled him to a deeper and safer portion of the nala as the terrorists, who had been stopped by Mushtaq's effective firing, now started firing short bursts with AK rifles. Nazir's sixth sense told him they were about to make a bid to break the cordon to escape.

Without caring for his safety, he crawled ahead, exposing himself and lobbed a grenade. He used a special technique to ensure that he would get both terrorists with one grenade. He pulled the safety pin and released the safety lever in his hand itself. A hand grenade's fuse takes four seconds to explode. Nazir threw the grenade after nearly two seconds and ducked. This way, the grenade was still in the air when it exploded. When exploding in mid-air, the shrapnel are more lethal and cover a wider area. The risk paid off. Both terrorists cried out as they were hit. On his signal, the soldiers rushed forward, firing from the hip. Both terrorists were killed on the spot. They were Afghanis, as suspected.

Nazir rushed Mushtaq to the hospital. There had been a lot of bleeding, but all his vital parameters were stable. Nazir breathed a sigh of relief. In the company, the company senior JCO praised his bravery in releasing the safety lever in his hand before lobbing the grenade. He wanted Nazir to be recommended for a medal. He replied simply, 'I didn't want the Afghanis to escape, not after shooting my friend. And as for the award, today I got the best award ever—my friend, the Maulvi is safe, Alhamdulillah!'

While narrating this incident to me, Mushtaq almost cried when he recalled how Nazir risked his life to save his in this encounter on 3 April 2001 in Mohammad Pora.

Nazir was also blessed with another prize. He had been encouraging his wife to join college and study further. However, before that could happen, something else was in store for the young couple. A son was born to Mahajabeen on 4 April 2001. Nazir and Mahajabeen were overjoyed. Her brother, Aijaz, named the child Athar. After a couple of months of confinement in her mother's care, when Nazir took his wife and son home, he surprised them by not returning to the Ikhwan camp but taking them to a house that he had bought from a friend. It was such a happy surprise for Mahajabeen. She said, '*Athar ke mubarak karam, aur Athar ke mubarak kadam* [Athar has brought us luck].'

Nazir's friend Zahoor told me how happy young Nazir and Mahajabeen were in their own house. However, Nazir often had to stay at the camp because of his duty. Mahajabeen was used to it and had adjusted well. However, when she saw his other colleagues coming home and not Nazir, she would not be pleased. He would always reply about the importance of duty. One day, she confronted him, and it was then that he told her that his Company Commander trusted him and Jahangir to guard the *kote*. A kote is a strong room where all the weapons and some critical equipment, such as the radio sets etc., of a unit are stored. Their main job was to ensure the safety and security of the kote in case of a suicide attack on the unit, so that the weapons would not fall into the hands of the terrorists. Such trust reposed in these former renegades was a big honour in itself. Despite her disappointment, Mahajabeen understood that her husband had earned the trust and confidence of his superiors through his hard work and dedication. She was a pillar of strength for him, a support so essential for Nazir to excel in every duty assigned to him. She was already showing signs of a good army wife.

There was an incident in 2002 in which Nazir showed an amazing presence of mind that saved the day and the lives of his colleagues. They were in Budgam on a routine patrol—often carried out to show presence in an area or establish contact with a source—when terrorists ambushed them. One soldier was killed, and another was wounded. The firing response from the army patrol was muted since there was no officer in the lead and the patrol had gotten demoralized because of the casualties.

Acting audaciously, Nazir fired a couple of grenades from his under-barrel grenade launcher (UBGL) and shouted, '*Army aa gayi, ab ghabrane ki zaroorat nahi hai* [The army is here now. You need not be afraid].' He gave a few other words of command and coordination instructions in a loud voice, giving their activities a larger-than-life air. He instructed someone to move with his men through the trees to outflank the terrorists. He sounded so convincing that the terrorists ran away; otherwise, the army patrol could have suffered more losses.

'He was always fond of carrying the heavy UBGL because he was so physically fit. I found it too heavy for me,' Zahoor told me while narrating the sequence of this operation.

On hearing this, I recalled something that I have been saying often to my colleagues and subordinates in the army: *Burdens are meant for shoulders strong enough to carry them.*

Chapter 6

The Rashtriya Rifles Wage War on Terror

The late 1980s were a difficult period in India's history. The country was dealing with counter-insurgency and counter-terrorism operations in Punjab, Jammu and Kashmir and several states in the north-east. Exacerbating it further was the involvement of the Indian Army in Sri Lanka. In response to the challenges, it was decided to raise a new force on the lines of the Assam Rifles, the oldest paramilitary force in India, which would be permanently located in the affected areas. This would also reduce the number of regular army deployments in counter-insurgency and counter-terrorist operations. Army units were normally rotated every two to three years, so it was believed that having a permanently stationed force would add to operational efficiency.

Rashtriya Rifles (RR) was the brainchild of Minister of State for Defence Arun Singh, and Chief of Army Staff Gen. K. Sundarji, in 1987, both scholarly individuals.

In 1990, six battalions were raised, along with two sector headquarters (each equivalent to a brigade) and a director general RR (DGRR) under an officer of the rank of a lieutenant general. Lt Gen. P.C. Mankotia was the first director general. Five out of the six battalions were deployed in Punjab.

The tasks entrusted to the RR are rear area security, counter-insurgency operations, maintenance of law and order, aid to civil authorities and augmentation of the field forces during war-like situations.

Seeing their efficacy, additional battalions of RR were raised for the Kashmir Valley and later for Doda District, along with necessary HQs.

While the idea of staffing the RR Battalions by ex-servicemen was toyed with, it was decided that the RR would be fully staffed by soldiers on deputation from the army.

RR played a stellar role in combating terrorism in Punjab. Encouraged by this experience, the Army Chief in 1994, Gen. B.C. Joshi, ordered the raising of additional RR battalions with requisite more sector headquarters and force headquarters (equivalent to a divisional headquarters).

The officers and men came on deputation from all regiments and corps of the army, with the majority being from the infantry. In raising the RR to full strength, they were provided with the best available vehicles, weapons and radio sets. In fact, RR units were the first to receive bulletproof jackets and specially designed Indian Army CI helmets known as bulletproof *patkas* (BPPs).

As a Major, I felt that soldiers posted from different battalions would lack in cohesion, motivation and camaraderie. However, I was happy to be proved wrong. The intrinsic strength of the army kicked in. With good leadership, a soldier's training and his motivation, they were shaped to strength in a new setting. There was an added advantage of providing continuity and contact with the terrain and the population, by virtue of being stationed permanently in the operational area.

Today, the company operating base (COB) of the RR battalion is a reassuring sight for the common citizens of the state. People vie to have a COB close to their homes, as it gives a reassuring sense of safety.

By September 1997, owing to the synergized efforts of the Army, RR, JK Police and other paramilitary forces, the situation in Kashmir had stabilized to such an extent that the army could de-induct a large number of troops including a few Brigade HQs from the Kashmir Valley over a two-year period. In fact, up to the spring of 1999, the army had already withdrawn a few battalions from the Kashmir Valley without replacements.

In 1999, there was a turbulent change in the Valley's dynamics with the start of the Kargil conflict with Pakistan. Army units and HQs located in the Valley were moved to the LoC in Kargil, and both the corps—15 and 16 Corps based in Srinagar and Nagrota, respectively—relinquished their counter-insurgency (CI) responsibilities.

The DGRR, Lt Gen. Avtar Singh, was moved from Delhi to Srinagar in June 1999 to assume command of the RR and operational control of rear areas. He was also appointed security advisor to the chief minister for CI duties and internal security., as the CRPF and the BSF were posted for security duties under the state police.

After the Kargil conflict, the DGRR returned to Delhi, and the two Corps Commanders resumed their additional responsibilities in CI operations. However, with the raising of a new Corps in Leh, army units that had moved up to Kargil got permanently deployed, and there was a need for more RR units. Therefore, in less than two years, several more RR battalions were raised under a few sector headquarters and force headquarters. The forces headquarters for deployment on both sides of the Pir Panjal Range were raised in September 1999 and January 2000, respectively. In 2003, another force HQ was raised to control operations in Udhampur district, which was fast becoming a transit route for terrorists between the LoC and Doda District.

The RR has come a long way in a short span of time. Starting with a token strength of six battalions when raised on 1 November 1990, it emerged as the largest counter-insurgency force in the world. The RR officers and men have acquitted themselves with bravery, courage and sacrifice, as testified by becoming the most decorated regiment of the Indian Army today with the maximum number of gallantry medals.

Chapter 7

LoC Watch: Command During Perilous Times

When I completed my tenure in Kargil in 1995, I rejoined my battalion as the second in command of the battalion in Port Blair, Andaman and Nicobar Islands. I served there for nearly three years. It was a good change and a great opportunity to learn about amphibious operations and working with the Navy, but soon I started missing the operational milieu of J&K. I was promoted to the rank of colonel in the middle of 1998, and I was appointed Commanding Officer (CO) of my Battalion in July, when it had just been deployed on the LoC in Poonch.

It is an interesting coincidence that our battalion was raised in Poonch in 1947 during its siege by the Pakistan Army for one year. In 1947, the Pakistan Army surrounded the Poonch town and garrison by occupying the mountains around it, as they outnumbered Maharaja Hari Singh's state forces. By the time the Maharaja signed the Instrument of Accession with India and the Indian Army could be sent to block invaders, the Pakistan Army had occupied key heights that dominated Poonch, a big town very close to the LoC.

However, one infantry battalion, 1 Kumaon, had managed to reach Poonch, led by a daring CO, Lt Col. Pritam Singh, before the siege was complete. He organized the defence of the town and garrison and mobilized volunteers to construct a makeshift airfield, which allowed the Indian Air Force (IAF) to open an aerial supply route. After the construction of the airfield was completed, many volunteered to serve with their personal weapons and ammunition. They were organized as Border Scouts. This later became my battalion. Several such volunteer forces had sprung up in the whole of J&K and were grouped as a paramilitary force called the J&K Militia.

Even as a voluntary group and later as a paramilitary battalion, my battalion played an important role in breaking the siege after one year. And in the golden jubilee year of the Poonch link-up, we were back at the same location, occupying the very same posts on the LoC that we had created in 1948. I had a very eventful and memorable tenure of three years as CO in Poonch District. We were deployed on the LoC.

Poonch lies to the south of the Pir Panjal Range in J&K, which separates the Kashmir Valley from the Jammu region. To the north in Kashmir, the army deployed more units in a robust anti-infiltration grid on the LoC and the RR units were in position to man the counter-terrorist grid in the hinterland of the Kashmir Valley. This combined effort led the terrorists to incur heavy casualties in their attempts to infiltrate and operate in the Valley.

In the late 1990s, this led to a discernible shift in the militants' attention to the south of the Pir Panjal Range. Several infiltration attempts were made by POK across the LoC in the Poonch and Rajouri sectors. The militants would attempt to use this longer route to go to the Valley or to Doda District, which was also fast becoming an active hotbed of militancy. Over the next couple of years, the frequency and intensity of engagement grew significantly.

In the army, there is a term for ambushing terrorists who try to infiltrate or when a gun battle breaks out when a cordon is established in the depth areas: it's simply called a 'contact'. In fact, the soldiers in my battalion used the colloquial word *taakra*.

In addition to our combat experience, many significant developments took place during the three years that I was CO of my battalion there: the nuclear tests of 1998, the Kargil conflict of 1999 and the Kandahar hijacking and its aftermath.

I was yet to assume command of my unit when India conducted the nuclear tests under the codename Operation Shakti on 11 and 13 May 1998. Consequently, Pakistan conducted five underground nuclear tests under the code name of Chagai-I on 28 May 1998. While India was already a nuclear state, these were the first tests for Pakistan, largely perceived to have been carried out with assistance from China. Several countries, led by the US, imposed economic and technological sanctions on India.

President Bill Clinton led the effort to unite several countries to apply pressure on both India and Pakistan against getting involved in a nuclear race. Several months of diplomatic activities and related dynamics followed and resulted in the Lahore Declaration in February 1999. Under the terms of the treaty, a mutual understanding was reached regarding the development of atomic arsenals and the avoidance of accidental and unauthorized operational use of nuclear weapons. The Lahore Declaration brought additional responsibility to both nations' leadership towards avoiding nuclear war as well as both non-conventional and conventional conflicts. However, it soon lost its sheen and meaning as the Kargil conflict started in May.

It was the first summer after our battalion assumed responsibility for our portion of the LoC. After the nuclear tests by both countries, infiltration attempts continued with renewed vigour. We suffered a couple of casualties too, but our boys acquitted themselves with bravery and élan. Soon, we were producing excellent operational outcomes and were effective in upholding our assigned tasks. The unit won the trust and appreciation of the hierarchy. There were other tangible and intangible benefits. Medals and awards won by our soldiers and officers were tangibles, and the combat experience gained by my soldiers was the intangible value addition, as was the spirit of camaraderie, enhanced by sharing risks and dangers together. Priceless! I have written a few stories based on my operational experiences during my tenure as CO in my book, *India's Bravehearts*.[12]

Recognizing the shift of focus to the south of Pir Panjal, additional RR forces were inducted in the area during 1998. Prior to that, we had to stretch ourselves to operate in the depth areas when some information about terrorists' presence was made available to our unit. As more RR units were inducted, it eased up our responsibility somewhat, and we could focus more on the forward areas. In mountains, troops are always at a premium, living up to the popular army adage 'mountains eat up troops'. To explain, when we deploy soldiers in mountains, you always end up needing more troops than you estimate because, when you go on the ground, you always find another peak or a spur that offers better control of the area and cannot be left unheld/unoccupied.

In May, we became aware of the infiltration in Kargil. The Pakistan Army had surreptitiously made some ingresses in areas on the LoC where the army was not deployed. The deployment over these rugged and high Greater Himalayan Range mountains cannot be continuous; there are unheld gaps, which are dominated by patrolling. By selecting their time to coincide with the winter when snow covers all the mountain tops and passes, the Pakistan Army occupied a few unheld mountain heights from where they could dominate and disrupt the highway between Srinagar and Leh. This is the lifeline for the Ladakh region; the only other, and lesser-used, road is the one from Manali in Himachal, which was a tenuous line of communication back then.

Operation Vijay was launched on 26 May to evict the intruders from Indian soil. Day after day, we would hear stories of attacks carried out by the army. By 26 July, the

---

[12] *India's Bravehearts: Untold Stories from the Indian Army* by Lt General Satish Dua, Juggernaut Books, 2020.

enemy had been fully evicted from Indian soil. This day marks Kargil Vijay Diwas, which is celebrated every year when a grateful nation pays homage to the Bravehearts whose grit and supreme sacrifice helped India win. There are so many heroic tales and so many heroes that it would not be fair to mention only a few names. In all, 527 soldiers and officers made the supreme sacrifice, and the officer-to-soldier casualty ratio was the highest in the world.

It may be noted that the conflict remained confined to Kargil. India also refrained from calling it a war. The IAF supported the army but did not cross the LoC. Among other things, mature statesmanship was clearly at work to ensure that matters did not escalate between the two nuclear-armed countries.

In Poonch, we did not directly participate in the conflict, so there was some professional regret in not being called on to join the high-octane operations, although we did get our share of heightened firing across the LoC, including artillery shelling.

The Kargil War had ended, but our vigil and operations on the LoC continued unabated. It was a bit surprising that infiltrators could find support and shelter among the locals when they had nothing to do with the Kashmiri cause. I used to discuss this with the local leaders and prominent citizens, including the MLA, G.M. Jan, and several others across the cross-section of society. My impression is that it had more to do with a mixture of religious sentiments and money. While most of the common village folk bore the brunt of terrorists' violence as well as hardships caused by restrictions imposed by the security force's operations, there were a handful who benefitted monetarily. Terrorists would often pay the locals for their safe passage, food and shelter in order to retain their trust and loyalty. They also paid a network of informers called over ground worker (OGWs). In most encounters, when we eliminated terrorists, we recovered large amounts of Indian currency. A decade later, when I was posted again in Poonch as the Brigade Commander, I was struck by the transformation: mud houses had turned into concrete three-storeyed buildings, and what used to be clusters of run-down huts had become small villages, complete with a mosque and a community centre. There was no indication of any legitimate economic activity to justify these transformations.

On 24 December 1999, an Indian Airlines flight from Kathmandu to Delhi was hijacked by five terrorists from Harkat-ul-Mujahideen (HuM), a terrorist group based in Pakistan. The hijackers landed in Amritsar for refueling and then proceeded to Lahore before flying to Dubai. In Dubai, they released a few passengers and the body of Rupan Katyal, who was the only fatal casualty in the entire episode. They ultimately flew to Afghanistan and landed in Kandahar, an area that was under the control of the Taliban. The hijackers were assured that there would be no raid on the aircraft. In Dubai, too, no raid was permitted by the authorities. The hijack showed the level of unpreparedness in India, and there was no convincing explanation for why no attempt was made to storm the aircraft in Amritsar.

The hijackers were demanding the release of three terrorists held in custody in India: Maulana Masood Azhar, Mustaq Ahmed Zargar and Ahmed Omar Saeed Sheikh. They were handed over in Kandahar by the Indian government on 31 December 1999. The remaining passengers and crew returned safely after a seven-day ordeal. This triggered another influx of infiltrators into J&K, most of which came under our area of responsibility.

Back in Pakistan, armed with global recognition, Azhar Masood launched a new terrorist group called Jaish-e-Mohammed (JEM). This group started specializing in suicide missions called *fedayeen* attacks. Interrogations of captured attackers later showed the modus operandi. Young men, mostly of unstable minds and often under the influence of psychotropic drugs, are tasked with carrying out the attacks. The very next year, in the first year of the millennium, they heralded their first attack against the Indian Army, when a suicide car bomb attack was launched at Badami Bagh Cantonment, the army base in Srinagar. The bomber was killed instantly and caused injuries to four army personnel and three civilians. The group's latest spectacular suicide car bomb attack at Pulwama in February 2019 was more deadly, in which forty CRPF men lost their lives. This outrage later led to precision air strikes at a terrorist camp at Jabba Top, near Balakot in Pakistan.

Terrorists' activities, which had registered an increase after the Kargil conflict, found even more currency in the following year after JEM was formed. This lethal escalation led to more RR battalions being raised, as we have read in the previous chapter. One day, I was pleasantly surprised to see my coursemate and friend, Col Lalit Chamola, walk into my unit. His announcement surprised me even more. He had arrived with a group of a few soldiers from the RR Bn that he was commanding, and the next day his entire battalion was arriving, consisting of approximately 1500 men. 'Where are you headed?' I asked, to which he replied, 'I have been tasked with setting up a second line of defence to counter infiltration and carry out counter-terrorism operations in the rear areas.' That was reassuring. 'Where will you stay?' I asked. His reply shocked me: 'You tell me.'

In the next few days, my unit and I assisted him to reconnoitre suitable areas for their HQ as well as company bases in the mountains. He himself shared my humble two-room abode for around ten days until their unit made other arrangements. Assisting them was an interesting learning experience, and more interestingly, when I returned there as

Brigade Commander a decade later, I could tell the officers how their HQ was set up. Another division-sized HQ was also set up in Rajouri District to coordinate the activities of RR battalions in the depth areas. I had learned that a similar HQ was also set up in the Valley in North Kashmir. The Indian Army was expanding the force raised to combat militancy in J&K.

Chapter 8

The Rise and Rise of Territorial Army (Home and Hearth)

A Bolder Experiment

Once the Kargil conflict was over, the nation slowly returned to normalcy. It was indeed a military and diplomatic feat that the conflict did not escalate into a full-blown war between two nuclear neighbours.

Leadership in India and Pakistan began to take bold steps to improve relations. Much is spoken about President Musharraf's famed visit to India, including Agra, in 2004. One of the steps that made a material difference to J&K was a ceasefire agreement across the LoC in November 2003. The LoC between India and Pakistan saw sporadic exchanges of fire between the armies, mostly triggered by the Pakistan Army's support of infiltration attempts by terrorists. It resulted in scores of casualties for the soldiers deployed on both sides and also caused loss of life and property to the people staying in close proximity to the LoC on both sides.

Elections for the State Assembly were held in October 2002. The National Conference emerged as the single largest party but lacked a majority. The People's Democratic Party (PDP) and the Congress formed a coalition government, with the PDP's Mufti Mohammad Sayeed serving as chief minister for the first three years and the Congress party's Ghulam Nabi Azad for the next three years.

It was at this time that the decision was made to wind up the Ikhwan and raise a Territorial Army (TA) battalion—Home and Hearth (H&H)—which these surrendered terrorist cadres could join. The TA comprises citizens from different walks of life who join their units for training a couple of months every year, and then they return to their vocations for the rest of the time. They form reserves to meet different needs or crises. TA soldiers have assisted in ecological ventures, combated terrorism and even run the Indian Railways during the railway strike in the 1970s.

A TA battalion (H&H) consists of sons of the soil who, by virtue of their knowledge of the land, language, people and culture, are able to generate intelligence, better connect with the locals and advise the army on relevant matters. The ex-Ikhwan cadres went a step ahead; they were aware of the way the terrorists operated and often knew some of them personally.

Initially, the Ikhwan cadres were reluctant to join the H&H battalion. Almost nobody came forward to join, as their leaders were holding back, undecided and uncertain. The police naturally wanted them to join as special police officers (SPOs). Rumours were spread that this battalion was a temporary arrangement, and that the army would employ them for the construction of the LoC fence. The rumours found resonance with the Ikhwan cadres because, at that time, the Indian Army was indeed constructing a fence all along the LoC to counter infiltration by terrorists. Over time, the rumours became malicious: once the fence construction was over, the army would kill them on the LoC.

But the army engaged with them and patiently explained its ideas about how the Ikhwan would be integrated into the TA battalion and how it was a long-term commitment. The initial misgivings and mistrust started giving way, and the cadres gradually came forward to enroll. Nazir, Zahoor and Mushtaq were among those who joined the TA as soldiers. Several cadres also joined the police and other paramilitary forces. Some, like Liaqat and Umar, did not join any of them.

Colonel Sudhir Tiwari was posted as the CO of the TA Bn (H&H). He was also the first person to report on 15 November 2003. He is an officer from my parallel batch from the Officers Training Academy (OTA) and we had done the initial training courses together. Lt Col R. Tomar reported two days later. He was second in command. The recruitment started at Anantnag High Ground with the help of another TA Bn (H&H). Recruitment also took place at Manasbal for North Kashmir. During my interaction with Col Tiwari, I learned that the raising of this battalion was unique and interesting in many ways, but also exasperating in some ways.

Not all those who were recruited were Ikhwanis. Next of kin or chosen relatives of Ikhwans killed or incapacitated while operating with security forces were also recruited, as were surrendered militants from different tanzeems, in addition to other patriotic youth.

Recruitment rules had been relaxed for the surrendered terrorists. Out of necessity, there was a one-time waiver on education and fitness standards, or medical tests. Almost all of them had seen combat, and some of them had bullet or grenade splinter injuries. There was one amputee too. Col Tiwari told me that a father–son duo was recruited together. Interestingly, the son was promoted to the rank of lance naik earlier than the father. So, Col Tiwari decided to give the father an unpaid promotion to the rank of naik to save him from an embarrassing situation. Nice improvisation on the part of the CO, and he had to resort to quick thinking on his feet several times for varied situations. Unusual challenges call for unusual solutions.

On 31 December, they moved to Dansal for training. Located midway between Jammu and Udhampur, Dansal has good training areas in the mountains, where the JAKLI recruits undergo training often.

The first fall-in was a strange sight. A formal muster is called 'fall-in' in the army. Most of the new recruits had long, bushy beards. In every physical training fall-in, in the morning, they would discover that anything between five and eight of the new recruits would be missing. They would have run away at night, as they found the disciplined life too much to handle, having been more rebellious and free willed in life thus far. Some returned, some didn't. The CO took a stand that anyone who absconded would not be accepted back. Their ex-commanders or ex-COs, with whom the Ikhwans had worked closely during earlier days, would ring up Col Tiwari, recommending their reinstatement. But they were rarely accepted again.

Col Tiwari believed that setting an example would have a salutary effect on others not to leave the training midway. His task was inherently tough—that of disciplining an undisciplined lot. In August 2004, I attended the Regimental Biennial Conference at the JAKLI Regimental Training Centre in Srinagar. There I had a chance to interact with Sudhir Tiwari about his experiences raising this unique unit.

The Ikhwans were not used to discipline or to the concept of taking orders from a chain of command. They were used to dealing directly with commanders and Commanding Officers. Battalion Havildar Major (BHM) Ali Mohammed Parray was one of the early TA recruits. He told me they rebelled against strict havildar instructors. During my chats with him, he seemed amused to recall that after a couple of days, he ran away from the unit only because he found the discipline too constricting. In fact, he ran away thrice during the training period. Each time, he was persuaded to return. After his third escape, he actually got caught during a raid conducted on a mosque by a RR Bn. Company Commander Maj. Chaturvedi took him to his CO, Col R.P. Kalita, who in turn took him to Col Tiwari. Col Kalita was later my brigadier general staff when I was the Corps Commander in Srinagar. He, too, had several interesting experiences to recount about the TA boys. He eventually retired as Army Commander of the Eastern Command.

Some of the ex-tanzeem commanders were given ranks according to their erstwhile standing, such as Pallay Khan, Mohammed Ishaq Mir, Mohammed Hussain Dar, Ali Mohammed Parry Hajin and Manzoor Ahmad Beg. A couple of years later, in 2005, when Mushtaq Ahmed Bhatt, aka Romeo, joined, he was given the rank of naib subedar, as he was the ex-commander of Pulwama and Shopian. Similarly, in 2006, when Sheikh Tahir, the ex-Commander of South Kashmir, joined, he too was granted the rank of Naib Subedar. These deviations from the procedures were made to accommodate the sensitivities and relationships between the leaders and the men. Later, men started getting promotions according to the promotion rules of the TA.

Making soldiers out of renegades was never going to be easy. Dealing with them with an iron hand would only harden these already battle-hardened men even more. Col Tiwari had to employ every trick in the book and out of the book to weld them together into a harmonious, cogent army unit. He had to synergize their individual capabilities into the operational machinery of a new experiment that he had set up.

These Ikhwans had their strengths too. They were extremely good at weapons training and field craft, and they were combat experienced as well. Most of them were agile and physically fit. Their contribution was significant, owing to their familiarity with the techniques and tendencies of the tanzeems as well as with the terrorists themselves. Nazir and his friends were happy to be in training and behaving as soldiers, not contra terrorists.

To get them to understand the ethos of the Indian Army, the spirit with which the soldiers serve and the ethos of camaraderie between soldiers, visits were organized for these new recruits to different army units all over J&K and right up to the Atari border in Punjab.

The Ikhwans-turned-TA-soldiers did not, however, stop throwing challenges at their leadership. Whenever faced with any strictness, they would call the CO or Sector Commander of the RR on their old Ikhwan connect. Once, they refused to do the Art of Living[13] course, saying that it would cast its magic on them. On another occasion, fifteen to twenty recruits revolted against the meals in their cookhouse. They threw down the langar food in protest. With a little probing, Col Tiwari discovered that they wanted only rice and no chapatis. The CO sat down with them and explained nutrition and the value of a balanced diet. He also asked for a couple of cooks to be recruited from the local dhabas to improve their culinary standards. Using every innovative trick in the book or out of it, Col Tiwari patiently bonded with and trained his men into an army unit.

All battalions in the JAKLI regiment have an MMG. This MMG is not the medium machine gun; it is the Mandir Masjid Gurudwara, all under one roof. It is a concept followed by all units of the regiment. Every Sunday, community prayers are held, and all soldiers, irrespective of their religion, go to the MMG and participate in prayers in all religions one by one with the pandit, the maulvi and the granthi. Even festivals have everyone participating together. We've had instances when, on Gurpurab, the granthi was not present and the maulvi conducted the proceedings. On Diwali, Muslim soldiers would volunteer to be on duty so that more Hindu soldiers got time off. Similarly, on Eid or during Ramzan, more Hindu and Sikh soldiers would reciprocate. This concept was started by Lt Gen. M.L. Chibber in the mid-1980s, when he was the colonel of the JAKLI Regiment. A Colonel of a regiment is

---

[13] The Art of Living was founded in 1981 by the world-renowned humanitarian and spiritual teacher, Gurudev Sri Sri Ravi Shankar. It offers numerous, highly effective educational and self-development programmes and tools that facilitate the elimination of stress.

considered the father figure or mentor of the regiment. In fact, this concept was eventually adopted by the whole Indian Army as *Sarv Dharm Sthal* (multi-religious prayer halls).

Col Tiwari wanted to introduce the MMG concept to his unit too, although the Hindus and Sikhs (largely tradesmen and clerks from other battalions) formed only around 5 per cent of it. By now, the CO had devised a way of sitting down with the men and explaining the reasons for doing things. As Ikhwans, they were used to assisting in intelligence generation or participating in operations but were never involved in unit affairs. Once they joined, these efforts to foster camaraderie were a new experience for them, and to everyone's surprise, they started appreciating this sense of belonging. After all, this is the essence of a soldier's pride—in his unit and his regiment. So, the CO explained the niceties of the concept of MMG. The men, who had known the abbreviation only as a medium machine gun, saw wry humour in the new twist. Gradually, the participation grew, including their participation in a Hindu *aarti*, during which the pandit explained the meaning and purpose of the aarti. Gradually, all festivals were being celebrated by all ranks together.

There were several instances of soldiers being killed or targeted when they went home on leave. Wherever feasible, Col Tiwari tried to send them to other places on leave, but this was not always possible. Whenever they had operational casualties, the CO and the unit maulvi attended every funeral. This stoked up a positive sentiment that these men, who earlier died like pariahs, were now being wrapped in the Indian tricolour and sent home along with a guard of honour. Once, the CO, accompanied by the maulvi, went to a village near Ganderbal to attend the funeral of one of their soldiers. The police warned them that terrorists were waiting to ambush the guard of honour and their team as they came for the funeral. It was a tricky decision. Col Tiwari persisted against all advice, and they quickly went in and were extricated immediately after the funeral. Such risky overtures always strengthened the bonds of brotherhood and helped them trust each other in operations.

While beginning any new venture, there is an understandable apprehension of the unknown. Col Tiwari constantly briefed his officers to focus on creating trust among the recruits. The TA recruits were very different from the young recruits in traditional army units, who join at an impressionable age and whose actions and attitudes are easy to mould. In the case of this TA Battalion, however, not only were these men much older, but their minds and biases were already made up. They had already seen more than a decade of combat. Everyone was hostage to his own experiences of combat and life in general.

The new soldier Ikhwans had their own challenges. The police tried to usurp this recruitment at lower levels so that they could work for them. The terrorists wanted to ensure that Ikhwan folded up since their involvement in operations was deeply hurting them. Other organizations, like the Jamaat-e-Islami (JeI), were highly sceptical about this TA battalion and thought it would not last; they spread many ungainly rumours about them.

On 2 January 2004, terrorists attacked Jammu railway station and killed seven passengers. A battalion of the JAKLI Regiment was stationed in Jammu and was tasked with launching an operation against the attack and preventing further loss of lives. Lt Triveni Singh was the first to reach the railway station with his quick reaction team (QRT). He immediately swung into action and ordered his troops to cordon off the station. In a swift action, Lt Triveni Singh killed the first militant and courageously followed the other, who was firing from the overhead rail bridge. Lt Triveni Singh knew that the militant could kill over 300 passengers who

2 Lt Satish Dua with a Kashmiri girl carrying a Kangri in 1980

Col Dua showing weapons and ammunition captured during encounters with terrorists to Defence Minister George Fernandes in 2000

Col Dua with CM Farooq Abdullah after Colour presentation
parade at Srinagar in 1998

Brig. Satish Dua visit to LoC at Poonch

Lt Gen. Dua with PM Modi, Governor N.N. Vohra and
CM Mufti Md Sayeed

Lt Gen. Dua with soldiers on LoC in Kashmir

Corps Commander 15 Corps Lt Gen. Dua on an LoC post

Opening the Zoji La Pass in 2016

Receiving Uttam Yudh Seva Medal from President
Pranab Mukherjee

Receiving Param
Vishisht Seva
Medal (PVSM)
from President Ram
Nath Kovind

Lance Naik Nazir Wani's wife, Mahajabeen, posthumously
receives his gallantry medal

Prime Minister
Narendra Modi
with Wani's
parents and wife
after presentation
of Ashoka Chakra

Nazir Wani during
Ikhwan days

Lance Naik Nazir Wani as TA soldier

Nazir Wani with his family

Nazir Wani being awarded Sena Medal by Army Commander
Northern Command Lt Gen. H.S. Panang

were vulnerable. Without waiting for the cordon to be fully in place, Lt Triveni Singh closed in and succeeded in killing the second militant too in a daring action, thereby averting a grave danger to the lives of innocent civilians. However, during the exchange of fire, Lt Triveni Singh got severely injured and succumbed to his wounds. For his extraordinary gallantry, unyielding fighting spirit, and selfless courage, he was awarded the Ashok Chakra posthumously.

In the aftermath of the attack, Col Tiwari collected his men and spoke to them about the special significance of the incident because it was one of the early operations by the sons of the soil from the JAKLI regiment. It was *their* regiment that successfully dealt with the terrorists. Honorary Captain Bana Singh, Param Vir Chakra, was invited for a motivational talk on that day. He had played a vital part in executing the highest attack in the world at an altitude of over 21,000 feet at Siachen Glacier as a part of his battalion, 8 JAKLI (Siachen). The new soldiers were riveted during these interactions and had several questions. It was evident that these men could relate to operations far better than training and discipline. When Sudhir Tiwari recounted this to me, I felt justifiable pride in my battalion, which had executed this attack at Siachen Glacier.

In March 2004, they returned to the Valley. Here they underwent induction training at the Corps Battle School (CBS) in the Valley for one month. Whenever any individual soldier or officer is posted to a counter-insurgency operations area, he is put through four to six weeks of pre-induction training. It is applicable to all newly inducted units as well. They are exposed to the nuances of the terrorism there and counter-terrorism drills and procedures. While all soldiers have had basic training, they need an orientation to the peculiarities of living and operating in operational areas. For instance, in such areas, all soldiers move out of their units with weapons fully loaded all the time. This is not the case in cities and cantonments. Repeated practice is required to ensure that carrying loaded weapons while moving around does not lead to accidental firing. Soldiers are introduced to local customs and sensitivities, which vary vastly between say, Kashmir and Manipur. They are practiced in counter-ambush drills, counter-IED (improvised explosive device) drills etc. Our soldiers did not require being exposed to all aspects. Their training schedule was amended accordingly. However, another Inf Bn TA (H&H), which was a regular TA battalion, also of the JAKLI regiment, and had been raised in Dana (Bihar), was also undergoing induction training in CBS at the same time. While both units comprised sons of the soil, Ikhwans were recruited only in one of the Inf Bn. The passing out parade for both the battalions was held together in CBS. The soldiers of the Inf Bn (TA) (H&H) which comprised of surrendered terrorists standing on parade were a far cry from the bearded and undisciplined brood that turned up in the early days of raising at the end of the previous year.

When his tenure came to an end, Col Sudhir Tiwari and his team had reasons to feel satisfied and proud of what they had accomplished. It is a unique unit of the Indian Army, the kind that has never been raised earlier and that we should never have to raise again.

With his mature and easy-going attitude, Col Tiwari also endeared himself to his soldiers. Once, he met with an accident while on leave. He was admitted to the Base Hospital in Delhi. Men used to call him to check on his welfare. Namaz was offered for him in the Battalion MMG, and they did *dua*[14] for him. In 2005, he handed over charge to Col V.S. Bhalotia, the new CO, and proceeded on two years of study leave. Such was the confidence that the soldiers as well as higher-ups

---

[14] To say a prayer for someone is called 'dua' in Urdu language. This is common in Islam.

reposed in Col Tiwari that he was brought back to command the battalion again after Col Bhalotia completed his tenure in June 2007. Col Tiwari commanded for four more years up to March 2011.

The TA colloquially uses the term 'terriers' to describe their soldiers. Thus, this Inf Bn TA (H&H) was endearingly nicknamed 'Kashmir Terriers'. It is common for army units to adopt an unofficial nick name, a prefix or a tag line.

The TA battalion raised, trained and sustained the TA soldiers. The TA unit by itself was not allotted any operational role. The soldiers were assigned (attached, in military parlance) to different RR battalions for the conduct of operations. In June 2004, four companies each were deployed with Kilo and Victor Forces of RR in North and South Kashmir, respectively. Men were, by and large, deployed as per their domicile. This way, they could generate more intelligence by keeping an ear to the ground, as the concept envisaged.

Nazir was attached to a RR Bn which was affiliated with RAJRIF Regiment.[15]

Having started young with the terrorists, he had earned his spurs with the contras called Ikhwans for nearly a decade, living on the edge but on the right side of the law. It was a gratifying feeling to wear a uniform and become a soldier in the Indian Army. As he reflected on his journey with satisfaction and pride, he was unaware that he was to attain greater heights that would make the nation proud of him.

---

[15] All RR Bns are affiliated to one or the other infantry regiment. This Battalion (9 RR BN) has 50 per cent troops from RAJRIF Regiment. The rest are made up from other arms and services.

Chapter 9

Nazir: A Kashmiri and a Soldier

Being a soldier was markedly different from being an Ikhwan. You had to be more disciplined and punctual all the time. You had to be on duty, whether you were in an operation or not. An Ikhwan joined up with soldiers mainly for operations. Disciplining renegades was not an easy task, nor was it an easy feeling for them either. However, their value in generating real-time intelligence and leading the operations remained unsurpassed.

Nazir felt that life as a TA soldier was much better. He felt the dignity and pride of the uniform. In his mind, he began to plan his life and the future of his family. He could also help his parents and brothers, as a soldier's salary was much better than what he earned as an Ikhwan. Their second son, Shahid, was born on 16 June 2005. The whole family was overjoyed, most of all Athar, the elder son. Nazir was assigned to a RR Bn along with his friends Zahoor, Amin and Mushtaq. They were pleased to be close to their homes and families. During that year, a new Company Commander, Maj. Paramvir Singh Jamwal, reported to the unit. He was a fine officer who quickly blended in with the troops. The soldiers also automatically trust such leaders and even blindly follow them in operations. Such officers form the backbone of the Indian Army. It was only natural that Maj. Jamwal would admire the bravery and dedication of Nazir, Zahoor and Mushtaq. A trusting relationship and both a professional and personal bond grew between them over the next decade and a half. The major trusted these men more than anyone else in all operations. One such operation started in 2005 and ended the following year, in 2006.

Chillai Kalan is the harshest period of winter in Kashmir. Beginning on 21 December, it is a period characterized by icy-cold weather, frozen lakes and more. Traditionally, there is a slowdown in activities during this period. But a soldier's life does not allow him the luxury of discerning harsh climates or difficult terrain. For him, duty is supreme.

At the end of the year, on 28 December 2005, Nazir and Mushtaq had gathered unconfirmed intelligence that a group of terrorists was somewhere in the general area and was waiting to make contact with someone. L/Nk Mushtaq Ahmad Mir (aka Maulvi) was Nazir's close friend and buddy since his teenage years; they had joined Ikhwan together and trusted each other with their lives. Later, intelligence reports confirmed that a group of terrorists had indeed sought shelter in Mantribugh village, Kulgam.

There was no time to think of the awful conditions during Chillai Kalan. An operation was launched by the RR Bn. The troops did not have intelligence about the exact location of terrorists, and in such situations, a cordon and search operation (CASO) is launched. A cordon was established around the whole village. Cordoning off a village requires a large number of soldiers. When specific information regarding the presence of terrorists is available, only a few houses or a mohalla need to be cordoned off. Not only does it require less manpower, but it also creates fewer hardships for the villagers.

After ensuring the cordon was effectively in place, the CO, accompanied by his QRT, reached the village square, where the village headman had been summoned. Nazir was with the CO. He spoke to the headman in Kashmiri, saying, 'We know that your village is harbouring terrorists. It may be that they have forced themselves on you under the threat of the gun. Please tell us where they are so that the poor villagers don't suffer any bloodshed.' The headman folded his hands and addressed the CO in Urdu, not Nazir: 'Sir, *Allah Tallah gawah hai, hamare gaon mein koi nahin hai. Hota toh mujhe zaroor pata hota* [As God is my witness, there are no outsiders in my village. If there were, I would have known].' The CO replied, 'Exactly, and that is why we began by asking you. If you choose not to tell us the truth, if there is any bloodshed, you will be responsible.'

All the villagers were gathered at the square, and the same questions were asked. Since no information was forthcoming, a search was started by seven different teams. In such cases, the soldiers announce through the village headman that they are looking for terrorists, and if nobody provides information about terrorists, then all villagers are gathered in a safe and central place so that soldiers can search the village. This ensures that if contact is established with terrorists and firing starts, the villagers are not harmed in the crossfire.

It was snowing, and there was over two feet of standing snow already. The search is a painstaking process. Soldiers have to search all rooms, below the beds and below the floorboards, below trapdoors, above the beams of the attic, where extra household items are stored, in barns and cattle sheds, in the compound and in the outhouse. And all this is done very tactically. It means that at every step of the search, soldiers are covering each other's movements as if the terrorists will start firing from the next room at any moment. This is a necessary precaution because when the terrorists are eventually discovered in their hiding places, they will come out with all guns blazing. The first soldiers are very likely to take the hit.

It is such a slow process that it is easy to lose focus and become casual. Carelessness in this situation can be very costly. The reader may wonder how a person can become careless when his own life is at stake. Ironically, it happens all the time. Staying in a situation long enough makes one dilute the attention—whether it is enemy shelling or firing, the person can get lulled into complacency. This search proved to be a long, drawn-out affair. It continued for five days; that must be some sort of record. To add to it, the operation started in 2005 and continued through the turn of the year. However, it was clear that the terrorists were hiding in the village. A couple of radio transmissions had been intercepted.

On the morning of 3 January, very few houses remained to be searched. The soldiers took a tea break. They joked that the sun would shine only after they wound up their operation. '*Chalo*, let's move towards the sun, then,' Nazir suggested, and, one by one, they all got up. Clearly, fatigue was setting in. The search recommended the same house where they had sat down for tea. Nazir's squad consisted of four RR soldiers, including him. As they were entering the house, suddenly there was a burst of bullets fired from above. Nazir, along with the three other soldiers, dashed to the ground. As they took cover and crawled ahead, the terrorist managed to pull the last soldier into the room as a hostage. Outside in the village, people started running away, and there was a lot of shouting. Some cows bolted across the street. More noises could be heard in the distance. In such circumstances, people are usually kept at bay. Whether it was due to the prolonged operations, the snowfall at the moment or both, people did start gathering and shouting across to check if the family in this house was safe.

It became a messy operation. The terrorists were positioned on a ledge on the roof. Nazir and two other soldiers were inside a room. The terrorists already had the upper hand because they were in a dominant position on the roof and had a soldier as their hostage. When one of the soldiers tried to break out through the window, the terrorists' firing from the roof was effective. He had to hastily withdraw back into the room. Nazir tried to inch towards the room in which they had dragged one soldier from their team. There was a burst of automatic fire from inside. Nazir had to crawl back to safety, and he was not happy about it. He wanted to free his colleague from the terrorists. Staying too long in the room was also fraught with danger, as the terrorists could set the room on fire by triggering incendiary ammunition or using a Molotov cocktail. The army also uses this tactic to smoke them out.

There was an open patch of nearly fifty metres that the soldiers had to cross in the open, where they would be vulnerable to the terrorists' firing.

Nazir executed a bold and daring move by showing great presence of mind. He sat at the window, facing inside. Suddenly, he leaned back out in the open, pointed his weapon above at the terrorist, and fired a rapid burst. The terrorists were taken aback and were forced to stay away from their vantage point. During this exchange, the other soldiers jumped out of the window and escaped safely. Nazir was the last to leave, only after all the others had.

While the impasse broke, the terrorists also managed to mingle with the locals and run away. The soldiers could not fire for fear of hurting innocent civilians. This operation began on 28 December 2005 and ended on 3 January 2006. No terrorists were caught or neutralized, but we lost a soldier who was taken hostage. However, because of his presence of mind and audacious action, Nazir managed to save three lives; otherwise, our toll could have been higher.

This incident highlights that these operations are not always successful. In fact, most of the time, we draw a blank. Either the information about terrorists is wrong, old or both. Sometimes, as in these cold January days, it is with difficulty that they are confronted, and yet they slip away. One may think it lowers morale. While it cannot be avoided, it also strengthens the resolve to avenge the soldier's death. It is this fire in the belly that keeps the soldiers going.

Nazir was very pleased that he had found a friend in Zahoor, who was like a blood brother to him. Mahajabeen, too, considered him a family member. She would even complain to him about Nazir's single-minded focus on his duty, at times at the expense of his family life. They were both posted in B Company, with Maj. Jamwal as the Company Commander. Once, during a lull in operations, they both went home on leave together. While granting them a few days of casual leave, Maj. Jamwal told them, 'I know you both like to be together, whether it is in operations or at home. *Yaaron ke yaar ho* [You are true friends]. I am impressed with your friendship.'

Only two days later, an operation started in the unit in the area of Puniwah. One of the hazards of living in the area itself is that you find out about such occurrences almost immediately. In fact, you get the information from both channels: the unit as well as the village. It is surprising how fast news travels in rural areas and in the mountainous countryside. Nowadays, everyone has a mobile phone. But even in the days before the mobiles, when I was a CO during the turn of the century, the spread of news in the countryside was amazingly fast. As soon as Nazir learned about this, he contacted Zahoor and told him that he was rejoining the unit so that he could participate in the operation. When Zahoor tried to dissuade him, he said, '*Main ghar pe chain se nahin rah paunga* [I will not be able to stay in peace at home].'

'Although the operation did not materialize into an encounter with terrorists, his spirit to be in an operation with his company remains etched in my mind,' recalled Zahoor while talking to me later. It showed that Nazir had a very well-developed sense of duty. In fact, Nazir had acquitted himself with courage and enthusiasm in all the operations in which he took part. His superiors had implicit faith in him. He was awarded his first Sena Medal in January 2007 for an operation.

The next year, the new Sector Commander visited their unit during Chillai Kalan. A Sector Commander is a Brigadier-rank officer who is like a Brigade Commander in the RR sector, which had three to four RR units. The Sector Commander had taken over recently and was coming on his familiarization visit. Whenever a senior officer visits, and interacts with the men, it raises their morale. It is an opportunity for the Company Commander to put forward his suggestions or problems. And it is almost customary to introduce to the visiting officer all the gallantry award winners or those who have excelled in operations or other fields.

Nazir and Zahoor were among those shortlisted to be introduced to the Sector Commander for their superlative performance after the briefing. They were all wearing their best uniforms. Nazir felt very proud when he wore his uniform, and, in his mind, he compared it to his Ikhwan days. Often, they did not wear uniforms for operations as they didn't want to give away their identity, but today he was dressed in the No. 1 uniform for the VIP visit.

During the winter, there is a general trend of an overall reduction in operations and incidents of violence in the Valley. Company Commander Maj. P.S. Jamwal was briefing the new Sector Commander, who had taken over the command of the sector HQ recently. Meanwhile, a source came to the Company Operating Base (COB) and informed Nazir that some terrorists were seen playing cricket in Awgam Village. Maj. Jamwal had just completed his briefing and was sharing a cup of tea with the Brigadier. Nazir cleared his throat and interrupted, '*Sir gustakhi maaf, ek zaroori khabar hai* [Sorry to interrupt you, Sir, but I have some important news].' Even the brigadier was listening with eager anticipation. They all knew that the only reason a soldier would interrupt his superior officers was likely to be the news of terrorists' presence. And Nazir did not disappoint.

Taking leave of the Commander, who readily encouraged them, Maj. Jamwal ordered his boys to get ready for the operation. He didn't have to specify anything more. Everyone knew what to do and what to carry in terms of weapons, ammunition, equipment, incendiary material, first-aid kits, painkillers and more. The teams muster a fall-in, as it is called in the army, where a headcount is taken, and the non-commissioned officers (NCOs) run a last-minute double-check for critical items.

As they rushed for the operation, as expected, no villager was ready to help in the small village that consisted of approximately fifty to sixty houses. Not being able to locate the house in which terrorists were hiding made their task that much more difficult. If terrorists could play cricket in the village, then it was likely that someone among them must have belonged to this village. After the cordon was established, their probing patrols made audacious movements towards some of the suspect houses, as informed by their source.

Nazir and Zahoor were probing a big house that was a little away from the others. They were moving cautiously, with one of them covering the other's movements. It is called a 'fire and move' tactic. Suddenly, they drew fire from one of the houses. They both dashed to the ground and crawled on their knees and elbows to take cover behind a half-damaged compound wall. An exchange of fire ensued, but the good part was that no one was hit in the opening round, and the terrorists had been localized. Soon, the Company Commander reached them. He crept forward to assess the situation. They observed all the doors and windows carefully, through which a possible entry could be made.

Leaving two other soldiers in their place, Nazir and Zahoor crawled back with Maj. Jamwal behind the safety of another house. Here, they discussed the plan to flush out the house. One suggestion was to set fire to the house. Nazir said, 'It takes years to make a house, and bringing it down affects the whole family.' He suggested a riskier option—use an IED to blast our way in, since it would be difficult to lob a grenade inside from a safe distance. He volunteered to throw in the IED, which carries more explosives than a grenade, but the risk lies in not being able to use your weapon for self-defence in the terminal moments, as he would be carrying the IED with both his hands.

A sporadic exchange of fire continued between the terrorists and the soldiers, who had taken positions in nearby houses or behind some other cover. At a pre-arranged signal, firing was intensified from a different direction by the soldiers to divert the terrorists' attention. This gave Nazir the opportunity, and he darted forward with the IED, ignited it by pressing the switch, threw it through a window with all his force and darted back behind cover, covering his ears with his hands. There was a huge explosion, and part of the wall was demolished. Dust and smoke blinded them all.

A few minutes later, when an assault team tried to enter the house through this gap, they came under effective firing from inside. The house was big enough for the terrorists to move to the rear portion and continue using their weapons.

Nazir had to repeat the operation with one more IED blast from the rear of the house. Now, the terrorists had nowhere to run. Four HM terrorists were killed in that operation. In this daring operation, Maj. P.S. Jamwal was awarded the Shaurya Chakra, and L/Nk Nazir Wani, along with two other soldiers was awarded the Sena Medal.

Zahoor joked with him after the operation, 'Yaar, I don't want to be so brave, but you always pull me ahead with you.' Soldiers like Nazir and Zahoor belong to two battalions. They were Territorial Army soldiers of an Inf Bn TA (H&H), who were also attached to a RR Bn for operational tasks. Both battalions justifiably take pride in them and their awards.

His parents and family, too, felt proud of his medal. Yet, in the villages in Kashmir, there are many who look down upon the local boys who are in the army, holding them responsible for the deaths of many terrorists whom they consider freedom fighters. The divisions in society in J&K run deep. Not many awardees, therefore, flaunt their medals like they do in other parts of the country. In fact, some of the sons of the soil face outright hostility. Nazir always had a great sense of duty, and the award of a gallantry medal stirred deep feelings within him. As a school dropout, his life took a dangerous path as a teenager, but he had the smarts to correct himself and join the Ikhwan in the nick of time. That was a decade and a half ago. Ever since, he had served enthusiastically and earned the respect and trust of his superiors and colleagues alike.

Nazir discussed this with Mahajabeen, and they spoke of their children's future. He wanted to ensure that his sons did not face any dilemmas or difficulties. Both the parents had plans for their sons: they wanted the eldest, Athar, to become an engineer and his younger son, Shahid, a doctor. Mahajabeen recalled later that he often told their younger son that when he became a doctor, he should treat poor people.

Together, they planned for a secure and better future for their children than the one they had.

Several years later, in 2013, a new CO was posted to take over the command of the RR Bn. Nazir was overjoyed to find out who it was—his earlier Company Commander in the same unit, Maj. P.S. Jamwal, was appointed as the CO on promotion to the rank of colonel. He asked for L/Nk Nazir Ahmad Wani and L/Nk Mushtaq Ahmad Mir to be a part of his QRT.

Serving in RR battalions is a tough job; your life is always at risk during operations, and you're away from your family for extended periods. While officers and soldiers were posted there for a term of two to three years, TA soldiers like Nazir were continuously deployed in operations, forever living on the edge.

Col Jamwal looked out of his office window. It was snowing. Only the soft hissing sound of the *bukhari* (traditional heater) could be heard. It was a Friday, an auspicious day. He was eagerly waiting to meet some of his old soldiers. It was around 12.30 p.m., and there was a knock at the door. His office runner came in and informed him that both of his earlier buddies had arrived. 'Send them in quickly. I am eager to give them a hug,' he said.

'Jai Hind, Sir. *Khushaamdeed,*' they both saluted. Wordlessly, Col Jamwal hugged them both one by one. He was overwhelmed. '*Theek ho na aap dono, aur aapke parivar bhi* [I hope the two of you are fine, and so are your families],' he inquired.

It was a sentimental meeting, and yet after some time, Mushtaq got up and requested the CO's permission to leave for his Friday afternoon prayer, or *Jumma ki Namaz.* Anyone else would have felt bad and taken offence at this impertinence, but the good Colonel said, 'I know that the 'Maulana' will have to go. Namaz cannot be missed.' They knew each other so well. 'Please do dua for Nazir, because I know he will stay back and talk to me. There is so much to talk about'. Mushtaq said, '*Yeh toh khud hi khuda ka banda hai*, Sir. *Naziri, batana sahib ko, aapne kaise apni jaan par khel kar meri jaan bachayi thi. Haan Sir, mere dil se toh iske liye hamesha hi dua nikalti hai* [He is the son of God himself, Sir. Nazir, you must tell Sir how you risked your life to save mine. Yes, Sir, my heart will always pray for him].'

Col Jamwal enjoyed his posting to this area, and it was good to be back with the operations and the people involved. He had an excellent working relationship with the soldiers. He maintained an air of informal camaraderie by greeting them with a hug and affording people like Mushtaq the courtesy of adhering to their religious rituals.

Chapter 10

Nearly Went to War Twice

In the 2000s, two high-profile terror attacks brought us to the brink of war.

Pakistan-based terrorist groups Lashkar-e-Taiba (LET) and Jaish-e-Mohammed (JEM) carried out a terror attack on the J&K Assembly in October 2001 and another one on the Indian Parliament in December 2001. India mobilized its armed forces on the Indo–Pakistan border. Pakistan followed suit and thus began a nearly year-long mobilization on the borders, the largest one since 1971. The world was worried about the disastrous consequences of two nuclear armies facing each other. The US played hardball. Pakistan President Pervez Musharraf publicly condemned the attack on the Parliament, vowed to combat terrorism and banned the terrorist groups in question so that India would not retaliate with an attack.

On 26 November 2008, the LET launched a terror attack in Mumbai from the sea route. It led to the deaths of 174 people, including twenty security force personnel and twenty-six foreign nationals. More than 300 people were injured. Nine of the ten terrorists were killed, and one was arrested. While India pursued diplomatic and political measures, no military steps were undertaken.

The terrorist groups and their handlers were continuously emboldened by our restrained responses to such high-profile attacks. Finally, it was in response to a suicide attack at Uri in 2016 that India launched a surgical strike across the LoC. The difference was in ownership. While Pakistan has always denied its involvement in the attacks by terrorists it sends across, the Indian Army announced to the world that we carried out this operation and our reasons for doing so. I was the Corps Commander in Kashmir then and will deliberately analyse it later in the book. Another similar air strike was launched three years later, in 2019, at Balakot, Pakistan, in response to another high-profile terror attack in Pulwama.

Brigade Commander

I was promoted to the rank of brigadier and was appointed Brigade Commander of the very same Poonch Brigade in which I had commanded my battalion. Prior to that, I was posted as the Indian defence attaché to the Embassy of India in Hanoi, Vietnam, where I had the opportunity to learn about the legendary guerrilla warfare tactics of the Vietnam People's Army as well as the Viet Minh. I visited their counter-insurgency training establishments and the famous Cu Chi Tunnels of the Vietcong, which were a great learning experience. I was also concurrently accredited to Cambodia and Laos, and these three years gave me a good understanding of the dynamics of Indo-China.

Having spent three and a half operationally active years in Poonch while commanding my battalion, I could hit the ground running and share with my brigade my experiences of the times when the violence levels and frequency of operations were much higher. The number of infiltration attempts and residual terrorists in the hinterland has reduced tremendously now. There has been a significant reduction in the violence levels over the last decade.

The year 2001, when I exited this sector after commanding my battalion, saw the maximum number of terrorists eliminated in J&K, and the only time that the number crossed 2100. During my tenure as Brigade Commander in 2009–10, I had very few operations against infiltrating terrorists. What made the difference? For one, over the last decade, there's been an issuance of much better enablers and equipment such as night vision devices, detection sensors along the fence, and radars for the detection of people walking on foot.

The biggest game changer, however, was the fence on the LoC. Colloquially known as the LC Fence, the army called it the anti-infiltration obstacle system (AIOS). When it was being erected in 2003 and 2004, I visited my own battalion, which was deployed in the depth areas of Poonch for a few months in the summer before it moved to Sudan to serve under the aegis of the UN. There, I learned of my unit's involvement in fence construction on the LoC. I must admit I was sceptical about this fence making a difference to the infiltration, as were many others who had operated in such areas. However, it is one of those situations where I am happy to be wrong. Over the years, with improvements in the construction of the fence as well as the sensors and other illumination enablers, the LC Fence proved to be a game changer in restricting infiltration. Even more, it channelized infiltrators to select areas, making it easier for the army personnel on the LoC to deploy the anti-infiltration grid with deadly precision.

This is not to say there were no residual terrorists operating in the hinterland. The RR conducted many successful operations against terrorists in the depth areas, although the numbers were significantly lower than earlier years. This was such a heart-warming sign. This situation was possible because of the years of operations by the soldiers of all units.

An interesting initiative of the Indian and Pakistani governments at Poonch was the Poonch–Rawalakot crossing point. It started as a small exercise a few months earlier under which there would be an exchange of trade and people twice a week at a designated place called Chakan da Bagh. The trade was conducted on a barter system and was restricted to a few items locally produced in J&K. People from J&K were also allowed to visit their relatives on the other side of the LoC with a special permit for a period not exceeding two weeks. One was always curious about the socio–economic conditions on the other side, and my interaction with the visitors from the other side often provided the opportunity.

During one such meeting at the crossing point, I had an interesting experience with an elderly man who was returning to POK after visiting his relatives on the Indian side. When we got talking over a cup of tea, I found him surprisingly candid. As he sipped his tea rather noisily, I asked him about his overall experience during these two weeks and how we could improve the arrangements. He told me he was very surprised at the gap between his impressions and what he saw during his visit. The general impression created in POK was that there had been no development on the Indian side of the LoC, Muslims were not permitted to offer Azaan (prayers offered five times a day using a microphone) at mosques, there was no freedom of movement and a whole lot of other canards. On the contrary, he found the Indian side significantly better developed, and there were no complaints about the freedom of movement or prayers. It validated what I had myself seen from mountaintops from where I could look across the LoC—the villages were well lit on the Indian side, but POK was comparatively dark. It was reassuring to know that the Chakan da Bagh experiment was productive, as people like him would go back and correct the perception even if they had a small footprint.

After commanding the brigade for a year and a half, I was posted to the Corps Headquarters in Nagrota, near Jammu, as Brigadier General Staff (BGS). My responsibility in this appointment was to coordinate the operations, operational-logistics, planning and training, inter alia, of the whole Jammu region. I could slip into this appointment seamlessly because of my familiarity with the whole area, the terrain and the operational scenario.

One of the major advantages of this posting was the constant interaction I had with the 15 Corps HQ in Srinagar, the Northern Command HQ and the Military Operations Directorate at the Army HQ. My interaction with other security forces, especially the police at higher levels, proved to be highly educational. It was my first time serving in a corps HQ. It gave me a good insight into strategic planning and policy making at higher levels as well as the new tactics that the terrorist and other separatist organizations had started employing in the Kashmir Valley.

That summer witnessed a well-organized stone-pelting campaign on a couple of issues as a new form of agitation inspired by the Palestine Intifada, which was successful in gaining worldwide attention. The separatists realized that unarmed struggle found more acceptance in the western world than an armed confrontation, and their belief was not unfounded. This forced the security forces to use anti-riot equipment such as tear gas shells and pellet guns. It gradually became a regular protest that would start in the mornings and end in the evenings (so that the boys could get back to their homes in villages after a day's stone-pelting). It was common knowledge that most of these boys were paid for their participation, and it was a good incentive for the poor to earn some money.

These protests were orchestrated mainly by the Hurriyat, who issued a calendar of protests, often at the behest of the other side from across the border, as it was found later. Over the past few years, the All Parties Hurriyat Conference (APHC) witnessed many ups and downs. The government and the Centre also gave it some space and engaged with it on occasions. This conglomerate cultivated links with Pakistan as well. Some of their leaders had also led a delegation to Pakistan. It held observer status at the Organization of the Islamic Conference (now the Organization of Islamic Cooperation). Their funds flowed from both.

Chapter 11

A Decade of Hope

It was 2011. A new decade had begun. Things were improving across the entire state, including Kashmir. Violent incidents were sharply down, tourists were on the rise and the fruit and handicraft industries were picking up.

Nazir took his family on a vacation to Delhi, Amritsar and Rajasthan to give them exposure beyond Kashmir. They experienced their first train ride. The boys were excited. Another place that left an indelible mark on Mahajabeen was the retreat ceremony at the India–Pakistan border at Attari–Wagah. The Indian and Pakistani soldiers lower the flags at sunset simultaneously. Since both armies still follow the British tradition right down to the tunes played by the bands, it is easy to coordinate their movements. Nazir explained to the boys how we were one country in the last century and how we are bitter adversaries now.

In addition to seeing many new places, they were able to spend quality time together as a family for the first time. It was a great bonding time. He promised his sons they would visit again.

In 2012, Nazir also bought a Maruti car for his wife to drive to school. It was a matter of pride for the family to have their own car. They made a family trip to the Sufi shrine of Dastgeer Sahib in Srinagar. It was a long drive, and they sought the blessings of the Almighty for their new car as well. In September 2014, the Kashmir Valley experienced unprecedented floods. It was the worst flood situation in over 100 years. The last such deluge was in 1903. Water levels at the Veshaw River in Kulgam, in the area of Sangam near Bijbehara or at the Jhelum were way above danger levels. In Srinagar, the bund protecting the city had been breached, causing heavy loss of life and property. Adding to the crisis was the partial breakdown of administration. Finally, a combined force of the army, the RR, the police, the State Disaster Management Authority (SDMA) and others were called in to launch combined efforts. As later events testified, the disciplined intervention, led by the army, saved the state from a ruinous calamity.

As the water levels were rising, Col Jamwal took Nazir along with him and started meeting people in different areas, reassuring them of assistance when and where required. Nazir called his father and checked on the family's well-being. He placed a similar call to his wife and inquired about the children. Nazir spoke matter-of-factly about the grave danger the floods posed: 'I may not come home for a few days. Thank God you all are in a safe place.' Mahajabeen had always been a pillar of strength for Nazir, taking care of the household responsibilities when he was caught up in his duties. Such support matters a lot for the soldiers. If there are pinpricks or pressures from the home front, then a soldier cannot give his best.

With water levels rapidly rising during the floods, the biggest initial hurdle was getting people to vacate their houses and move to a safe place. Nazir accompanied the CO during these trips. The village elders' help was sought to convince the villagers to move. It required tact, persuasion and a bit of coercion to get them to agree.

It was not smooth sailing everywhere. In several parts of the Valley, it was difficult to convince people to vacate in time. Attachment to property is hard to overcome. Col Jamwal's boys used a combination of persuasion and force to get things done, and Nazir played a big role in it. When the crisis was over, it drew great appreciation from the common folks, some of whom were deeply apprehensive earlier. The district commissioner (DC) recognized their service and organized a formal function to thank them. Col Jamwal accepted an appreciation certificate on behalf of his jawans. Nazir was present at the function as a member of the CO's QRT. He was also felicitated by all present.

Nazir felt emotional. It was not only the public's appreciation but also the commendation from his unit. The experience of helping the local folks with issues other than security and countering terrorists was a novelty. Working with other agencies and volunteers for a humanitarian cause to save homes and lives was a profound experience.

The flood experience also showed Nazir for what he was—a sensitive, well-rounded personality and a good human being empathetic to others' problems. Having come up the hard way, he wanted to ensure that his near and dear ones did not have to face the hardships he did. He would always assist his wife with housework. He used to say, 'Ghar wali ke liye kaam karne mein kya sharam [There is no shame in helping one's wife].' He never raised his voice at his wife. One day he said to her, 'You should leave your job, and we will settle down in Jammu.' Mahajabeen teased back: 'Haan, at least then you will not be able to leave me and run away to do your duty whenever an operation starts off in your unit.' This was because several times, when he was on leave and heard an operation was starting in his unit, he would voluntarily resume duty.

But when he was home, he liked spending time with his sons. He himself was not given to physical exercise that much, yet he always encouraged his sons to play games. He was fond of chess and loved playing it with them. He would say to them, 'Yeh dimaag ka khel hai [This is a game for the brain].' Another quirky and endearing trait was his fondness for cartoons, and nothing gave him more pleasure than to spend time with his sons, playing chess or watching cartoons on TV. Yet another favourite stress buster for Nazir was playing video games on his mobile phone.

He was also concerned that the youth of his beloved Kashmir were being misguided by vested interests and that the mobile phone was the biggest tool being used for radicalization. He explained these things to his sons so that they wouldn't fall prey to false propaganda or hate sentiment. Nazir was very concerned that his sons, the children of a soldier, should not go astray. His own experience had taught him how easy it was to slip down a path that only brought misery and suffering.

As an apt reward for his humane qualities and his professional soldiering, he was selected to serve in Sudan for six months under the aegis of the UN along with another battalion of the JAKLI regiment. It was a matter of honour to be selected; it was a different kind of exposure and the deputation allowance was generous.

Chapter 12

International Peacekeeper: Nazir

The saga of Nazir's bravery and courage was not limited to his expertise in counter-terrorism operations in India alone. He displayed similar traits while being deployed overseas as an UN Peacekeeper in war-torn South Sudan in 2015.

Another battalion of the JAKLI regiment, my own regiment to which Nazir also belonged, was an exemplary battalion and had earned a very good name for itself during the Kargil War in the Batalik Sector. The Battalion was awarded numerous individual gallantry medals, and the unit was awarded the Battle Honour of 'Batalik' for their outstanding valour and sacrifice. Battle honours are awarded to a unit for displaying great valour and sacrifice during war. In 2014, the battalion was selected to serve as a part of the UN peacekeeping force in war-torn South Sudan.

Nazir was then still a rifleman (Rfn) who had been awarded the Sena Medal in 2013. On the basis of this achievement, he was chosen to be part of this JAKLI contingent earmarked for peacekeeping operations under the aegis of the United Nations Mission in South Sudan (UNMISS). For this purpose, Rfn Nazir Wani was posted to his new battalion in August 2014 for a challenging overseas mission in this forlorn part of sub-Saharan Africa. It was a matter of great honour for Nazir to be selected as a member of a peacekeeping force. For someone who had started his life as a terrorist against India, the irony of being selected as a peacekeeper to represent India abroad was not lost on him. He thanked Allah for the great honour and vowed to serve his motherland with utmost dedication.

He joined his new unit in New Delhi as the battalion was preparing to be deployed overseas. Like him, there were a few more soldiers selected from other battalions of the regiment who had been posted to this unit for this peacekeeping tenure. After a couple of days, all these soldiers were called for interviews by Commanding Officer Col Pushpinder Singh Choudhry. He started by congratulating them: 'Congratulations for being selected to join our Bn for this UN deputation to South Sudan. While it is a matter of pride, it also places a huge responsibility on your shoulders. You are ambassadors for your battalions in my Bn. Welcome to the Bn. From now on, this is your battalion, your new home. Later, as you proceed to South Sudan, you will all be ambassadors of the Indian Army and the country in a foreign land, where you will also be working with soldiers from other countries in your UN mission. Remember, it is difficult to win so many awards, as you have won or our battalion has won in Kargil, but it is more difficult to maintain the high reputation that comes with such awards. I am sanguine you will always keep the battalion flag flying high. Best of luck, Jai Hind.'

These sentences had a profound impact on Nazir. He was acutely conscious of the fact that he had started on the wrong side of the law and was a disruptor of violence. Today he was singled out for a peacekeeping effort between warring factions, some of which may not be very different from terrorists' outfits. He made a silent resolve to act and behave in a manner that did his new *paltan*[16] and his regiment proud.

He longed to make his officers—those who trusted him so much—proud. Always.

In 2015, South Sudan was not only the poorest country in the world but was also facing a severe humanitarian crisis due to the civil war since 2013. The genesis of the war was an intense rivalry between the Dinka and Nuer tribes in the quest to gain ultimate control of the ruling government. President

---

[16] In the Indian Army, soldiers endearingly refer to their battalions as paltan, a carry over of British days.

Salva Kir (Dinka) and Vice-President Riek Machar (Nuer) had both formed their respective armies and were fighting for control of tracts within the country. Over 4,00,000 people had perished in the civil war, while several million were internally displaced.

The unit was inducted into this melee with a mandate to ensure the safety of the internally displaced persons (IDPs) and facilitate talks between the warring factions. The battalion had a four-point deployment, spread across 400 km of the hot and arid South Sudanese plains. One company was deployed at each deployment point.

Rfn Nazir, as part of Charlie Company, was deployed at Melut, a small oil-rich town on the bank of the Nile River, which was inarguably the most difficult location in the UNMISS. The company had a mission to protect about 14,000 IDPs dispersed in motley settlements made out of tarpaulins and co-located with the company garrison.

On 19 May 2015, the Sudan People Liberation Army (In Opposition) Rebel Army launched a massive attack on the Sudan People Liberation Army (SPLA) Army garrison in Melut with the INDBATT (as the Indian Battalion was known, in the UN Peace Keeping Forces) company location and the IDPs being caught in the direct line of fire. The C Company was the only part of the UNMISS deployment that stood its ground and refused to be evacuated to ensure the safety of the IDPs. For three days and three nights, the company held its ground and occupied positions in a protective cordon around the IDPs. Rfn Nazir stood out as an exemplary and courageous soldier, who despite the heavy overhead firing, volunteered to be part of the close IDP protection team.

In the face of continuous overhead and direct firing by the deadly Sudanese rebels, he took initiative and evacuated several injured IDPs to a place of protection. For three days and three nights, he seldom sought relief and displayed grit and courage to a very high degree. C Company of the JAKLI Bn received accolades from the highest levels due to the grit displayed in the face of enemies in a foreign land, and Nazir's contribution to this achievement was unequivocal. His comrades as well as his superiors recognized his experience in combat and his dedication to service.

The above incident highlights a very important facet of Nazir's personality. He was a true soldier to the core and had an insatiable allure for operational tasks in the face of the enemy. He had absolutely no regard for his personal safety and held his regiment, his Indian Army and his country paramount in all his decisions and actions. By virtue of his combat experience, Nazir was a great asset during this mission, his CO told me unhesitatingly.

Chapter 13

The Kashmir Year

In 2015, I was promoted to the rank of lieutenant general and appointed as the General Officer Commanding (GOC) of the Srinagar-based 15 Corps. This placed an onerous responsibility on me for the entire army in Kashmir, the security of the LoC as well as the operations in the hinterland. It was a coveted honour for any officer to be selected for this post, as this was the most operationally vibrant corps of the Indian Army, with maximum troops under it.

Most people fly to Srinagar. Some, however, prefer travelling by road from Jammu to enjoy the verdant beauty of the land. However, I began my tenure by undertaking a motorbike trip with my two sons from Manali in Himachal, over the Rohtang Pass via Ladakh (there was no tunnel then), and especially drove along Pangong Tso Lake, where there is no road, reliving old memories, through Kargil. This was the same route on which I drove a Jonga in the Rohtang Rally in 1984. It was an energizing and educational experience to see the changes over time. The 50-km drive along Pangong Tso Lake from Chushul to Lukung is the same place where the Indian and Chinese armies have been facing each other since May 2020. This drive through Ladakh from the Himachal side via the Rohtang Pass gave me a good understanding of the Ladakh region, where I had served two decades earlier.

It is good to have an understanding of the neighbouring zones, and ground reconnaissance is more effective than helicopter reconnaissance. To the south of Pir Panjal was the Poonch Rajouri region under another corps, where I had served multiple tenures, including being the Brigadier General Staff (Operations) at the Corps HQ. Hence, my understanding of the neighbouring corps zones was good.

There were several new aspects to Kashmir when I assumed charge. The Valley was just coming out of reconstruction after the floods the previous year, which had caused heavy loss of life and property. On the political front, there was a coalition government in the state formed by the People's Democratic Party (PDP) and the Bharatiya Janata Party (BJP). The former had won majority seats in the Valley and the BJP in the Jammu region. There was hope that, by aligning with the party in power at the Centre, this coalition would be able to deliver on the carefully crafted 'agenda of alliance'.

My Kashmir tenure of a little over a year was characterized by some defining events. This period witnessed the change of chief ministers owing to the demise of Mufti Mohammed Sayeed and the elimination of top leaders of all three major terrorist organizations, notably Burhan Wani of HM, which led to unprecedented violence in the valley. Then there was the terror attack on the army camp at Uri, where we lost eighteen soldiers, and it led to the surgical strikes ten days later, which became the inflection point for India's changed response to high-profile terror attacks. The air strikes on Jabba Top near Balakot were a testimony to the shift in operational paradigm.

There were, however, two new facets or big changes I saw that merit mention. In 2014–15, it was common to see young boys waving Pakistan flags or black flags in congregations or protests; their faces were invariably covered with a veil. It was almost a fixture after Friday prayers, reported dutifully by the media. Just before I assumed charge, Burhan Wani changed all that. He and his friend caught everyone's imagination by posting their pictures on Facebook with their faces uncovered and holding weapons. Adroit use of mass and social media was made to create a Robin Hood-like image for him. It was plain to see what was happening. The anti-infiltration grid proved to be rather effective in the last decade, and the number of residual terrorists in the valley had fallen sharply; those who were left were unable to exfiltrate to POK for training. So they came up with another stratagem: a proactive use of social media as a force multiplier. Social media was also widely used to mobilize crowds for stone-pelting before, during and after operations against terrorists. In fact, social media became the primary means of radicalization. The other side had cleverly changed tactics and provided the tools to make good use of the technological enablers, in keeping with the times. In the early stages, the state's response to the changed tactics was not very effective.

However, one could also see that while the separatists continued to issue a calendar of protests regularly, their hold over the youth was slipping, and control over their activities was tenuous. The new young terrorist leaders would openly warn them against the consequences of allowing the entry of the Islamic State in Iraq and Syria (ISIS) and al-Qaeda into the state. They also did not heed his calls on various occasions. A year later, one of the new terrorist leaders, Zakir Musa, even threatened to behead separatist leaders, including Syed Shah Ali Geelani, the ageing president of the APHC.

Another new development was using stone-pelting incidents to provide cover for terrorist operations, making them an effective force multiplier. They were used to distract the security forces during an encounter by opening another front against them, where even women and children were employed. This alerted the terrorists and, at times, even helped them escape. In the 1990s, when security forces entered an area for operations, locals would lock themselves indoors, totally avoiding contact with armed troops. Now they were rushing to meet them with stones. A complete tactical turnaround.

One of the first things I did was pay a courtesy call on the Governor and the chief minister. Governor N.N. Vohra was a very experienced, polished and articulate man. As he had years of experience in Kashmir in various roles, including that of defence secretary and home secretary while I was in service, interacting with him was a great learning experience. Since 1993, J&K had a Unified Command HQ under the CM, and heads of security forces and intelligence agencies were members. I personally did not agree with the term 'Command HQ', because it did not have any command authority and was more along the lines of a coordinating mechanism. The Corps Commanders were security advisors in their respective areas. There were a few occasions when I felt duty-bound to fulfil the role of security advisor to the CM.

Mufti Mohammed Sayeed was an astute politician and a gentle person. He was always courteous and soft-spoken, almost paternal. I remember once asking for a meeting to discuss something important. It was during the run-up to Bakr-id, a month or so after I assumed charge. Mufti Sahib welcomed me and offered Kahwa, the traditional Kashmiri herbal tea laced with saffron.

After initial courtesies and a bit of small talk, I launched into the purpose of the visit. Communal passions had been aroused in the state. There had been a few cases of public cow slaughter in South Kashmir, which had inflamed passions in the Jammu region. A Kashmiri truck driver had been lynched by a mob in Udhampur. I cautioned the CM as his security advisor that he must use his political heft to stop the disturbing incidents in public and also figure out a way to remove the videos circulating on social media. Nothing in South Kashmir could happen without the support of the Jamat, and that was their constituency.

I appraised the J&K context by giving an example from the north-east, where I had my last command as a major general. Any agitation in Nagaland hurts people in Manipur, as the only viable road that leads to Manipur passes through

Nagaland. I told Mufti Sahib how the Nagas exploited that as a pressure tactic.[17] I stated plainly that if the Jammu–Udhampur region started disrupting the only lifeline of a road that serves the Valley, it could make things difficult for the people here. He caught on immediately and promised to look into the matter. We ended the meeting with him teaching me how to enjoy the exotic Kashmiri bread sheermal by dipping it in kahwa and eating it before it became too soggy.

Geelani issued a statement the next day asking for restraint and harmony in the spirit of the religious festival. Kashmir has extremely complex dynamics, with layers of power play and wheels spinning within wheels. And there are too many stakeholders: political parties, religious organizations, separatists, terrorist tanzeems, universities, madrassas, media, bar association, the human rights groups, the business community, NGOs and civil society. Surely, I must have omitted some of them.

I laid emphasis on creating good synergy among the army, the central and state police forces as well as intelligence agencies. In all these organizations, attitudes percolate from the top downwards, so if there is coordination at the pinnacle of the pyramid, it transmits down to the base. In line with this ethos, I worked on building a good working relationship with the top levels of these organizations. At that time, this rapport-building exercise involved Director General of Police (DGP) K. Rajindra Kumar, head of IB Harmeet Singh, Additional Director General of Police S.M. Sahai, Inspector General of Police (IGP, Kashmir) Javaid Geelani, IGPs of the CRPF and the BSF and other intelligence agencies. This synergy paid off in several situations. Consequently, the Core Group meetings that

---

[17] EXPLAINER: Why the Nagaland-Manipur Arterial Highway Had Been Closed for 10 Days'. Wire, n.d., https://thewire.in/politics/explainer-nagaland-manipur-highway-blockade.

I chaired as the Corps Commander were also effective in coordinating our efforts.

At the end of October 2015, the dreaded district commander of LeT, Abu Qasim, was eliminated in a meticulous and well-planned operation in South Kashmir. I single out this operation because a few days earlier he had killed Sub-Inspector Altaf Dar of the J&K Police. He was infamously known for an attack a couple of years earlier in which we lost twelve army soldiers and many more were wounded. He was a Pakistani national who carried a reward of Rs 20 lakh on his head.

A couple of days later, I went to the Company Base of the RR Bn to compliment the boys who had conducted the operation. I congratulated Col P.S. Jamwal, the CO and his team. I also met Col Akhil Mende, the CO designate. While meeting the brave soldiers who participated in the operation, I was introduced to the JAKLI TA boys, who had been at the forefront. This included Rfn Nazir Ahmed Wani. He was still a sepoy, called a rifleman in some regiments, such as mine. Our meeting was full of warmth, especially since we were from the same regiment. It was a matter of supreme pride for them because, for the first time, the Corps Commander in Kashmir was from the JAKLI Regiment. Little did I know that I had just met a hero who would make the regiment and the country proud, and I would be writing a book on him later.

The Jammu and Kashmir Regimental Training Centre in Srinagar is the only Training Centre in an operational area and has to participate in operational duties such as road opening, patrolling and protection with convoys or VIPs. While this is an additional strain during training, it also gives young soldiers invaluable experience and confidence. Having my Training Centre under my command as Corps Commander as well as colonel of the Regiment was a unique experience for me as well as the regiment. It also enabled me to see closely the problems my troops faced as sons of the soil. It was at this time that I thought of writing the story of Ikhwan, the bold experiment of a TA unit of surrendered terrorists and the inspirational story of the raising of my regiment as a voluntary force during operations.

The JAKLI regiment is unique since it was raised as voluntary force during 1947–48 when Pakistani army-backed tribal intruders attacked in order to capture the state. Several volunteer groups sprang up to resist them in different parts of the state, which were later amalgamated into a paramilitary force called J&K Militia. In 1972, it was converted to a regular regiment of the Indian Army and renamed JAKLI in 1976.

In most parts of the country, the army lives secluded in cantonments, training and honing its skills for modernization of warfare and whatever it takes to safeguard the territorial integrity of the country. But in border states or areas where law and order or the security situation is precarious, a well-coordinated rapport with the civil administration, the police, other security forces, intelligence agencies, other organs of the government and the local people is very important. This was the foundation of my strategy, and I kept reminding my HQ and the formation commanders under me not to ignore this vital dimension. Such an approach paid rich dividends in due time.

Even though the violence levels were gradually declining, it was always noted that the youth who were injured in police action were always young men around twenty years of age, certainly below twenty-five. The nagging question always was how no one in his thirties or forties ever got injured in violence on the streets. During my interaction with different sections and different strata of the population in different parts of J&K, it had been my impression that while it is the youth that participates in terrorist activities, protest, stone-pelting and everything in between, the blame does not squarely lie on them alone. They are mostly from poorer families and are radicalized and motivated by vested interests to indulge in violence, whether armed or without weapons. The children and grandchildren of the leaders who incite them are not part of the street agitations because they are usually studying or working at a safe, faraway place in India or another country. Several such stories come out in the media from time to time. So, in effect, these terrorists are also our misguided children.

Those below thirty are the so-called 'children of the midnight knock'. Since the late 1980s, it has been the children who have borne the brunt of terrorists' violence and suffered the inconveniences caused by security forces operations and curbs imposed by the administration. They have grown up with these restrictions. Hence, the children are soft targets for terrorists, separatists and the ISI, Pakistan's notorious spy service.

If normalcy had to return to the state, it was clear to me that we needed to focus on the mind space of the youth, take the negative fissiparous thoughts out of their minds, and fill it with the idea of a peaceful and all-embracing India. Like I explained to soldiers that not every Kashmiri with a beard was a terrorist, the youth needed to be oriented to the idea that not every soldier with an AK rifle is an enemy.

As an extension of this thought process, several programmes and schemes aimed at engaging with the youth in a positive manner were initiated. Massive recruitment drives, the Super 30 programme, wherein we helped prepare candidates for all-India competitive entrance exams and national integration tours where a group of youth were taken to different parts of the country to show them the progress and highlights of other places. As a first, I insisted and arranged one such tour for girls too, which drew great enthusiasm but also attracted trolls in the media and social media. Of course, the negative reaction was used to highlight the medieval mindset in some sections of their society.

In order to have a more meaningful engagement with the youth, we started sixty-six youth clubs across the Valley called 'Chinar Nau-Jawan Clubs' under Operation Sadbhavna (goodwill), which provided a place for the children or youth to meet with each other and utilize facilities such as the library, internet access, gym, indoor sports and other recreational activities. The one in Anantnag even created a go-karting track, which was a big hit. These clubs became very popular. Gradually, NGOs and corporates stepped in to provide vocational training and, in some cases, even placements when they realized that the army was providing a safe and ready-made interface with an enthusiastic section of society.

Once, the Joint Director of the IB informed me that Pakistan had long been practising their philosophy of 'death by a thousand cuts'. But the latest inputs they had picked up were that the deep state of Pakistan was moving towards a philosophy 'death by thousand revolts' to be adopted for spreading discontent in all parts of the country to tie down the security forces, cause casualties and generally sap morale. Come to think of it, the frequency of such protests across the country has increased, and their reach and viciousness have increased manifold through the adroit use of both mainstream and social media.

Reconstruction and rebuilding after a devastating flood in the Kashmir Valley in 2014 were a prime focus of the administration. Appropriate attention was also being devoted to preventing the recurrence of widespread devastation. I made a suggestion to the CM, Mufti Sahib, that he should project a case for a TA battalion (Ecology) for cleaning the water bodies and de-silting of the Jhelum. This would recreate capacity for the run off water during monsoons. This would also generate employment opportunities for the local youth, and any measures that keep them off the streets with stones or weapons in their hands should be encouraged. He was enthusiastic about the project. However, Mufti Sahib passed away before it could progress further. He was 80.

After Mufti Sahib's death on 7 January 2016, the PDP could not decide on his successor easily. It took three months for his daughter, Mehbooba Mufti, to assume office, which she eventually did on 4 April. In June, she contested the Assembly by-election from Anantnag and won as the sitting CM.

Chapter 14

Nazir's Saviour Act

In 2016, Nazir was promoted to lance naik. The pay raise is not worth mentioning, but there is recognition of merit and status enhancement among peers. Gainfully using the extra foreign deputation allowance earned while serving with the United Nations Mission in South Sudan (UNMISS), Nazir bought a plot of land on the outskirts of Jammu for his family to eventually settle there, as he had planned all along.

On 14 November 2017, an operation took place in the area of Qazigund in South Kashmir. If you've travelled to Srinagar by road, you will remember that Qazigund is the first town you hit when you reach the plains of the Valley after descending from the Pir Panjal Range. It is almost a ritual to stop there for a tea break en route to the Valley.

The operation was led by the CO of the RR Bn, Col Akhil Mende, himself. Nazir had always been a part of his QRT, just like Jamwal, his predecessor. Going by the intelligence report available, initially three villages were cordoned off, which took the better part of the night. Later, the LeT terrorists were localized to one village called Qund. During the operation, as the cordon was being re-established around Qund, the terrorists started suddenly firing with AK rifles from a couple of houses. As the gun battle started, the soldiers took cover and engaged the terrorists with fire from every possible direction. In such circumstances, it is important to ensure that soldiers don't fire at each other. Col Akhil trusted Nazir with this important responsibility so often that Nazir started crawling from man to man to reassure them and say a few words of encouragement and advice to a few new ones. He would say, 'Fire a single shot when you can. Conserve ammunition.' Or simply, 'Don't

worry, we have them surrounded. They can't get out. Keep
cool.' L/Nk Sushil Kumar told me later, while recounting
this operation, that Nazir knew no fear. '*Uske saath rehke
hamara bhi darr nikal gaya Saab* [Operating with him made
us lose our fear too].'

A few terrorists were killed during the firefight, but
suddenly someone shouted that the terrorists had made a
break towards the adjoining forests. Col Akhil Mende quickly
issued a fresh set of orders. He didn't want the terrorists to
blend into the shadows of the forest, making it impossible to
spot them. Time was of the essence. The cordon was lifted,
and the operation was turned to focus on the search. Breaking
into small groups, the Rashtriya Rifles (RR) soldiers started
searching the forests. CO Col Akhil Mende, L/Nk Sushil
Kumar and L/Nk Nazir Ahmad Wani were together. At one
stage, they had to cross a fence. Sushil took position with his
AK rifle, and Nazir crossed first, followed by the colonel. As
Sushil crossed the fence, Nazir spotted some movement out
of the corner of his eye. Instinctively, he pushed the CO to
the ground and fired a quick burst. There was one retaliatory
burst. It was a providential action of Nazir that the CO, Col
Mende, be pushed out of harm's way. Sensing that the bullets
were fired from behind a huge rock, Nazir crept up to the
rock, and before anyone could react, he attempted to skirt
the rock from the precipitous higher side, which would not be
a natural choice to negotiate. He was hoping to surprise the
militant. However, they were both surprised to find themselves
in such close proximity.

Nazir saw him first. The terrorist's back was towards him,
as he was facing away, but not for long. Hearing the rustle of
undergrowth made by Nazir's movement, the terrorist turned
to face him. Nazir recognized him. It was Muzamil Ahmad
Dar, the Lashkar-e-Taiba (LeT) district commander. Taking
advantage of Nazir's moment of surprise, Muzamil dashed to

the ground and fired his rifle. It wasn't aimed properly, and the bullets flew harmlessly. Nazir, however, was more focused. Years of combat experience came to his aid. He dropped to a knee and steadily fired a long and steady burst at the terrorist. Muzamil was hit but went down, firing wildly. Nazir ducked them well and rushed to see if Muzamil could be given first aid. But it was too late. It had literally been a case of fastest finger first. And it was that close! In that operation, four terrorists were eliminated with no casualties to our own troops.

For his undaunted courage during the operation, Nazir was selected for the rare 'Bar to Sena Medal' in the Independence Day 2018 list of gallantry awards. This honour is extremely prestigious because the awardee gets the same medal for a second time.

As the events were to turn out, by the time of the investiture ceremony in Northern Command HQ at Udhampur, Nazir would not be alive. It was his wife, Mahajabeen, who would receive the award. She must be the only soldier widow to receive two gallantry awards on behalf of her husband within a fortnight, one of them the highest in the country, awarded by the President in front of the nation at the Republic Day Parade less than two weeks later.

Chapter 15

Momentous Moments:
The 'Karara Jawabs'

Burhan Wani was a HM commander who represented a shift in tactics from 2015 onwards. He and some of his cronies posted their pictures on Facebook, posing with weapons in their hands rather than hiding their faces and identities. They drew pleasure from broadcasting their deeds. The most common image etched in people's memories is the one of him posing with a sub-machine gun on Facebook. He and his team had been eluding the security forces' dragnet for a long time.[18]

Burhan's handlers had made adroit use of mainstream and social media to create a Robin Hood-esque image for him. He had become somewhat of a cult figure for the separatist-leaning youth of the Valley. Hardly a week would go by without a video clip of him going viral in the Valley. Sometimes, it was a terse warning to locals to stop supporting security forces, a caution to girls to dress modestly or a threat to J&K Police to stop hounding terrorists. This was being skillfully planned by his handlers across the LoC. Once, there was even a clip of him playing cricket. The local media was often complicit in creating this larger-than-life image. Sometimes, a news article about him would be accompanied by a huge half-page picture of him staring down from the front page for an effective perception impact. Like the youth all over the world, the young men of J&K were also hungry for an icon, and they found one in Burhan Wani.

But it was only a matter of time before all his terror came to an end. The wonderful synergy that had emerged among

---

[18] 'Kashmir's Disturbing New Reality: The Young Militants of Kashmir', *Hindustan Times*, n.d., https://www.hindustantimes.com/static/the-young-militants-of-kashmir/.

the army, the police and intelligence agencies led to a gun battle in Kokernag in south Kashmir in July 2016, in which Burhan Wani was shot dead. The swift and quick gun battle between the RR soldiers and terrorists bore mute testimony to the fact that Burhan and his ilk were high on image building and low on training.

In the aftermath of his death, the Kashmir Valley witnessed unprecedented violence with daily protests, stone-pelting and *bandhs*. Although these protests had been anticipated, the violence and vehemence were unprecedented. A large number of young boys would get injured by pellet gun fire or tear gas. The occasional fatalities added fuel to the fire. The situation of protests and violence in the Valley was so bad that the CM used to review progress every night at her residence, 'Mayfair'. Present in the meeting were heads of all the security forces and intelligence agencies, the Chief Secretary, the Home Secretary, the Divisional Commissioner and a few more. We apprised the CM of the day's violence graphs and generated the plan for the next day. Decisions regarding curbs for the next day would be made. It took almost two months before matters were brought under control.

The late-evening gatherings were almost like the Unified Command HQ meeting, except the approach was more hands-on. The army and RR units continued to dominate their areas, but controlling mobs and violent stone-pelting was essentially the responsibility of the police and the CRPF. The violence on the streets was increasingly causing more loss of life and property, and the group had to collectively convince her to take stronger steps. Each organization also used its own channels to convince Delhi that additional efforts were required to control the situation in the Valley. For the army, the task was relatively easy to handle since reinforcements could be sent from the southern parts of the state itself. Home Minister Rajnath Singh made a hurried trip and was briefed by all the security forces. He followed this up with late-night meetings with the Governor and the CM separately.

This was one of the few times I witnessed how the police, and by extension, the CRPF, came under political pressure. In the army, when a situation turns bad, we allow it to stabilize before making the accountability count, unless it is inescapable. There should be no hurry for 'heads to roll' to show action. This is because, after all, those in higher positions know the problem more intimately. Any immediate changes in leadership may prove disastrous. However, here one senior police officer was sacked, and another barely survived.

Violence control measures are never a pretty sight. Curfews that cause hardships to common people, frequent shutting down of mobile internet and the use of anti-riot equipment to disperse the mobs, of which the maximum damage is caused by the pellet guns, are all part of the endeavour. However, these harsh measures were necessitated to control the violence on the streets, which was resulting in the loss of innocent lives and property.

During these troubled days, I closely observed the interplay between the political and administrative decision-making processes. They left me deeply unimpressed and often disturbed. The administration in Kashmir suddenly seemed to have gone to sleep and was in an absent mode at a time when it should have been functioning on all cylinders. Even earlier, during the initial days of the Kashmir floods in 2014, I had heard this was what would happen. And such slumber mode was not restricted to any particular department or administration since it cut across party lines and personalities. I remember a particular incident when a blood donation camp was organized at the SKIMS Hospital. Food packets and other aid items were sent for the patients and their families, but there was no one from the administration to manage their distribution. Some separatist cadres exploited the opportunity in front of the media and acted as if they were the intended benefactors. It was then that I realized that the army needed to get fully involved, down to the last level. The army is trained to be ruthless in implementation, but it is also constantly oriented to feel the pain of those who suffer and deal with them with empathy. That is what makes the Indian Army the preferred choice for responding to major emergencies.

The scale of violence spilling out on the streets got the attention of the nation and the world media. The Kashmir Valley saw hectic political activity during the summers. I personally interacted with several high-level delegations. Home Minister Rajnath Singh visited at least three times. He was accompanied by Rajiv Mehrishi, home secretary, who also visited separately. An All-Party Parliamentary Committee also reviewed the situation. I still recall that the separatists refused to meet with them. Besides, there were several other delegations, NGOs and media teams. I briefed most of them myself. The Army Chief visited several times and the Army Commander more frequently to make a first-hand assessment of the situation. During this period, I also interacted with the late Dineshwar Sharma, director of the Intelligence Bureau (IB), who played a vital role not only in generating intelligence but also in shaping the opinions of those who mattered. He later returned to Kashmir as the government's interlocutor for J&K.

An incident concerning the media merits mention. Once, a well-known media personality interviewed me on the current situation—one of my many interactions with the media. The team was going to the government hospital to gather sound bites of the youth injured in tear gas and pellet firing. I suggested to them that it was only fair that they also get a reaction from police and CRPF personnel who were injured because of stone pelting, so that both sides could be represented, and they agreed. I spoke to DGP K. Rajendra Kumar, who agreed. However, when the media team reached the police establishment, they were not given access. I got a call from the media anchor that they were running out of time, as they had to file the story by a set deadline, and they were not getting access to the injured policemen. I then gave them access to a couple of wounded policemen who were admitted to the Army Base Hospital at Badami Bagh Cantonment. In all likelihood, no one was doing it deliberately; after all, the DGP had personally agreed. But most organs of the government were unable to grasp the urgency or importance of presenting our side of the story. Either that, or there were vested interests at play. There were wheels within wheels everywhere. In this day and age, perceptions shape the environment. It is not the police alone; the army too was rather closed and hierarchical about interaction with the media and enhancing its presence on social media. Whereas mass and social media are nimble, agile and spontaneous with the advantage of a flat organizational structure, the security forces are vertical and find it difficult to engage with others. This aspect does need a fresh look, or we will pay a huge price in the coming years. I am happy to note, however, that things have improved vastly since my days as the Corps Commander.

During that summer, we witnessed rampant violence and stone-pelting was taken to the next level. Around the beginning of the decade, when organized stone-pelting started, it was confined to the highways. The young men would come from nearby villages, indulge in pelting stones and return home by evening after getting paid. But now it was being seen in rural areas too. Another interesting fact was that the boys participating in it were getting younger; some were even as young as ten and would be spotted frequently. Stone-pelting was not new to Kashmir. I remember in 1984, when I was posted in Kupwara, when there was a power failure in the middle of the night during the Olympic Games and a hockey match was being watched on TV, people would come out of their homes and start throwing stones at the transformer in the street. Symbolism of stoning the Satan?

In 2016, one could see that while the separatists still issued a calendar of protests regularly, their hold over the youth was slipping, and control over their activities was tenuous. The brash young leaders would openly warn them of the consequences if they opposed the entry of the Islamic State in Iraq and Syria (ISIS) and al-Qaeda. They also did not heed his calls on various occasions. A year later, Zakir Musa would even threaten to behead separatist leaders, including Syed Ali Shah Geelani.

It was such an irony that the leaders' own children and grandchildren were either out of harm's way in other locations or enjoying government service, but they would incite the local youth to risk their lives and limbs by participating in protests, stone-pelting and terrorism. Such was the level of radicalization. Another interesting insight was that hardly anyone over their late teens or early twenties was ever injured in protests or stone-pelting. Surely, if the whole Valley was aggrieved, why were only youngsters participating in such protests?

I noted that the separatists and other vested interests were always quick to close schools and colleges as a part of the protest calendar. This provided them with a ready pool of youth available for participation in their protests. Also, if any new government schemes were to be promulgated to engage with the youth, schools should be the starting point. The closure of schools would preclude that as well.

Here I wistfully recall a couple of incidents that seemed surreal to me. While in Srinagar, I once flew in a Sukhoi-30 fighter aircraft of the Indian Air Force and I also did a skydiving jump from an Advanced Landing Helicopter

(ALH) from 13,000 ft, without any formal training. Both of these were exhilarating experiences in themselves, and I was overwhelmed by the beauty and the heaven-like serenity of the Valley as experienced in the air. The stark contrast it made with the strife on the ground hit me the moment I landed on terra firma. A couple of years later, as chief of IDS, I returned to JAKLI Training Centre as Colonel of Regiment for a unique affiliation parade between JAKLI, INS Kochi of the Indian Navy and a squadron of the Indian Air Force based at Srinagar. Then I had flown in a MIG 21, and had a deja vu feeling, as earlier.

I always felt that Kashmir needed more dynamic leadership. It has a rich cultural history and many facets to be proud of. It could have been driving the growth story of India with its tourism and handicrafts, but it went the wrong way. Icons across the world are increasingly younger. Here, the younger leaders did not inspire confidence. That could be one of the reasons for the runaway popularity of renegades like Burhan Wani among the youth.

The civil society should have played a stronger role. I used to discuss this with a few Kashmiri friends. Children knew only stone-pelting as an expression of protest. My questions to them were: how long before they do that in their own homes? Was society going to implode? The elders and teachers must take charge. One of them told me that anyone who tried would risk his or her life. Maybe that was it. For years, the army, the police, the CRPF and other forces have sacrificed their lives to improve things in Kashmir at all levels. So, civilians didn't get involved. Whether it was Punjab or the north-eastern states, peace could only return when civil society was fed up with the violence, started speaking up against it, and began assisting the forces.

I even discussed this with Dr Karan Singh, the last regent of J&K. He was a veritable storehouse of knowledge, and it was an enriching experience to interact with him and his family, especially his son Vikramaditya, who was a People's Democratic Party (PDP) leader back then, and his wife Chitrangdha, a very gracious lady. Once, I was discussing the situation with them at a discreet social gathering at Karan Mahal on the famous Gupkar Road. Ghulam Nabi Azad was present as well. They agreed with me about the need for civilians to get more involved. However, soon our discussion turned to whether Donald Trump would become President of the United States. That was when the incongruity of it struck me—the discussants and the topic in the unlikely setting of a place where its own turmoil was so rife.

I was due for a promotion to Army Commander on 31 August 2015. However, it was only logical that my tenure would be extended until the situation was brought under control. I wouldn't have been happy to leave mid-stream either. A logical timeline, to my mind, was the Darbar Move[19] to Jammu, which was scheduled for 27 October. It is then that the focus shifts to Jammu. Besides, the onset of winter slows down the tempo or frequency of operations, both at the LoC as well as in the hinterland.

Uri and Surgical Strikes

While the protests and stone-pelting incidents were reducing and things were getting under control, suddenly, terrorists struck at Uri. A suicide terrorist attack at our army base very close to the LoC killed eighteen soldiers. It was a major blow on my watch. I was seething with fury and frustration. It was a dark Sunday for me, 18 September 2016, which I will never be able to live down, as I lost eighteen young lives during my

---

[19] Srinagar is the summer capital of J&K and Jammu is the winter capital. The state government offices move between the two cities accordingly, which is understandably a big exercise in itself, and is colloquially called darbar move.

command. Earlier that year, a similar attack took place at the Pathankot Air Base. There were many such incidents in which we were always on the receiving end. We could only increase our defensive measures. It was time to put the enemy on the defensive.

The senior military leadership had already arrived and been to Uri to take a stock of the situation before receiving the top government functionary who landed that afternoon, He wished to go to Uri to see things for himself, but I strongly advised against it. Fires were still burning, and sanitization operations were in progress. I recommended that we go to my office for a detailed update. At my Badami Bagh Headquarters, I briefed him on a map in the operational room. Senior military hierarchy was also present. Kashmir was my area of responsibility, so the onus of briefing was on me. Once the general briefing was over, he asked me, '*Toh ab kya karna hai* [What do you plan to do now]?'

I suggested that only the close group move to my office for further discussion on the future course of action. Once there, senior officers spoke first, discussing larger plans and possibilities at national level. They talked of various contingencies and our preparedness to meet them, including the possibility of our response spiraling into something bigger. I did not say anything. It was their role to work out the higher plans and possibilities at the national level. I was in charge of the operational domain only in Kashmir and could only suggest the operational response.

There was widespread outrage in the nation against Pakistan based terrorism. Taking a firm stand against it was crucial for which swift action was deemed necessary. The nation demanded a decisive response and addressing this issue became a priority.

We needed to go across and the LoC and hit the terrorist camps inside their territory.

It was agreed that such a stern response was necessary. Senior leadership issued only two directives to me. First, there should be no collateral damage (by steering clear of inhabited areas) and second, to ensure no casualties among our own soldiers. Though achieving the desired end state of the above two directives cannot be guaranteed in times of war, we had to make our best efforts to ensure the same.

A more detailed account can be read in my book, *India's Bravehearts.*[20]

After hitting the targets, we would announce our actions to the world, unlike Pakistan, which denies its involvement in terrorist strikes. The operation required meticulous planning and coordination, overseen by senior leadership, with progress reviewed periodically.

On 18 September 2016, when our base at Uri was attacked, the UN General Assembly was in session, and the terrorist attack drew widespread condemnation globally. Pakistan was isolated. Prime Minister Nawaz Sharif's speech in the UN General Assembly was scheduled for 21 September. From that point of view, Pakistan's timing of the terrorist attack at Uri was flawed. There was international pressure on Pakistan to stop supporting terrorism, with an active push from our diplomats. Our foreign minister, the late Sushma Swaraj, was scheduled to speak on 25 September. We decided to let that day pass peacefully. We also ensured that we did not launch any operations for the next two days in order to lull the other side into complacency. Meanwhile, during these ten days, we continued to show routine movements and operations all along the front.

Terrorist launch pads are usually one or more houses in a village right on the LoC, from where they observe the movements of our patrols for a couple of days, familiarize

---

[20] *India's Bravehearts: Untold Stories from the Indian Army* by Lt General Satish Dua, Juggernaut Books, 2020.

themselves with the terrain, and then launch an infiltration. However, the actual terrorist camps are a few kilometres inside. Here, the element of surprise was absolutely crucial to the outcome. The trickiest part was passing through their forward line of defence. Forward defences (groups of posts) on both sides are protected by minefields.

What also helped us was the fact that the Pakistan Army was unprepared for infiltration from outside. They were not used to situations in which we carried out such manoeuvres. While the Indian side is trained to deal with infiltrators and thus deploy ambush parties and use other such measures, the Pakistani side was more static and focused largely on manning the LoC posts.

Fortune favours the brave. We did not have a single casualty while causing heavy losses to the terrorists. The Pakistan Army tried to downplay the losses and even claimed that no such strike took place and that they encountered only heavy firing across the LoC. A metric of the success of our operation was that, from 2016 onwards, they started deploying soldiers to guard against a possible repeat of our surgical strike. The 'uncertainty' mode has been reversed towards them.

The Director General of Military Operations (DGMO), Lt Gen. Ranbir Singh, held a press conference and announced to the world that we had hit terrorist camps across the LoC. He also announced that we had no desire to escalate the situation and that the Pakistan DGMO had also been told this over the telephone. The media used the term 'surgical strike', and the name stuck. It merits mention here that while there have been shallow operations across the LoC in the past from both sides, what was different this time was the scale and depth of the targets and that we owned up to it proactively. It was also the first time that we used diplomacy as leverage for an operation. For instance, we had built public opinion against the terrorist strikes at Uri by using the UN General Assembly as a forum.

The grief of losing eighteen soldiers in Uri cannot be overcome, but the surgical strikes gave us a sense of closure.

This turned out to be one of the most important events in my military career, where I could salute the memory of the departed by working with the Bravehearts who executed the surgical strike. This operation showed the world that India had the capacity and resolve to execute a hot-pursuit type of operation at multiple points. It also set the stage for precision air strikes at Jabba Top near Balakot, Pakistan, in 2019, when a suicide car bomb attack resulted in the loss of forty CRPF personnel in Pulwama, Kashmir.

A month later, I was promoted and moved to New Delhi as chief of Integrated Defence Staff to the Chiefs of Staff Committee (CISC). As the Colonel of the JAKLI Regiment, I continued to remain in touch with my troops and battalions, frequently visiting the JAKLI training centre as well as the Corps HQ until my retirement. Just as I was fortunate to sign off my operational experiences on a high note of being the Corps Commander in Kashmir during tumultuous times, including the surgical strikes after the Uri tragedy, similarly before retiring as chief of IDS, I had the proud privilege to steer the construction of the National War Memorial near India Gate from the design selection to the execution stage. Having been in combat and lost several comrades, it gave me great satisfaction to give shape to a befitting tribute to the fallen heroes of the Indian Armed Forces after independence.[21]

It would be remiss of me if I did not mention some other important stakeholders in this fight against terrorism. Let me begin with this interesting story.

---

[21] Arman Khan, 'Independence Day: 7 War Memorials in India That Will Fill You with Pride', *Architectural Digest India*, August 14, 2022, https://www.architecturaldigest.in/story/war-memorials-india-you-must-visit-that-will-fill-you-with-pride-and-patriotism/.

Chapter 16

If You Get There Alive, You Will Live

If you get there alive, you will live. Isn't that a fantastic motto for a hospital to live up to? And this is not a marketing tagline coined by the hospital; this is the perception that all soldiers in the Kashmir Valley have about the Base Hospital in Badami Bagh Cantonment, Srinagar, where my HQ was also located. This hospital receives more trauma patients than those suffering from lifestyle diseases. Trauma cases normally bring to mind images of road accidents and burn-related wounds or injuries. At this hospital, they see fewer road accident injuries and more gunshot wounds, landmine blast casualties, grenade splinters, rocket and artillery splinter injuries and more. They see fewer patients with diabetes and heart ailments and more of those suffering from hypothermia, high-altitude pulmonary oedema, frostbite, chilblains and such.

Soldiers are deployed on the LoC with Pakistan, where casualties of the type described above are an occupational hazard. But over the last three decades or more, the terrorists' violence has increased the violence levels manifold on the LoC as well as in the hinterland in the beautiful Kashmir Valley. And the Base Hospital evokes this kind of sentiment in the soldiers posted in Kashmir. *If you get there alive, you will live.* That's how good the hospital, its medical care, the dedication of its doctors and staff and its reputation are.

It's also a high expectation to live up to. And those who are posted to that hospital get caught up in that ethos and find themselves willingly wanting to keep up the good work.

As soon as the helicopter carrying a casualty takes off from the area where an operation is going on, a siren is sounded and people start converging to their action stations: doctors, surgeons, anaesthetists, nurses, nursing assistants,

151

the ward staff, support staff and more. The Base Hospital is not contained within just one building. Since it is in an operational zone, they are always overworked and have to work at odd hours. Despite the extra work and extra hours, they put in, they are all very patient with the patients.

During my command tenure there, we modified an Advanced Landing Helicopter (ALH) as a makeshift ambulance. So, whenever an encounter with terrorists or an operation started off on the LoC or in the hinterland, the medical component was mounted on the chopper. It consisted of the equipment, apparatus and medicines that would be required for gunshot wounds and splinter injuries in a hurry; a medical officer flew along, and by administering medical aid to the casualties right from the get-go, when they arrived at the evacuation helipad, we could save a lot of patients because the medical aid provided during the golden hour is vital to saving lives. Speaking of helicopters, I recall that during our younger days in operations, we could evacuate a casualty by helicopter only during the day. So, the casualty had to be on the LoC, or the area of operations, until the next morning, as most operations took place at night. Sometimes the weather would play truant during the next play. So, depending on the situation, we would often start evacuating the casualty by land route, which involved carrying him down physically in a stretcher over hours of walking, and then by ambulance after reaching a road. In 2016, ALH helicopters Mark 2 were inducted in the Valley, which had night-flying capability. Now, casualties could be evacuated 24/7. That was a boon for the soldiers—a reassurance that wasn't there before. But it made the medical warriors work around the clock. And they never complained; they were happy that they could save more lives.

Once, after a particularly violent operation that resulted in quite a few casualties, I went to the helipad to meet the soldiers. As they were being transferred from the helicopter to the ambulance, I noticed a young soldier with multiple gunshot wounds who had lost a lot of blood but was conscious. I said to him, '*Himmat rakhna beta, sab theek ho jayega* [Be strong, son. You will get well soon].' He replied, '*Ab koi darr nahin, Sahib, main to toh yahan zinda pahunch gaya hoon, ab toh jeeyunga bhi, aur phir se ladunga bhi* [I am not afraid now, Sir. I have reached here alive. I will live to fight another day]!'

This prompts me to place on record another important facet.[22]

The insurgency and terrorism in J&K were not fought by the fighting soldiers alone, which largely comprised the Infantry and RR soldiers. There are several supporting arms and logistics services that support and assist the effort. Without them, it would be impossible to succeed. We just read about the medical services and the aviation corps. Similarly, Artillery operated the unarmed aerial vehicles (UAV) for reconnaissance and surveillance; engineers defused bombs and improvised explosive devices (IEDs); Army Intelligence Corps provided valuable inputs and sometimes even participated in operations; Army Service Corps and Army Ordnance Corps provided the logistics and the electrical and mechanical engineers repaired and maintained all weapons, equipment and vehicles, to name a few. All of them together carried out road opening duties, which involved searching for explosives laid by terrorists and ensuring the safety of military and civil vehicles from terrorist attacks.

---

[22] India's Bravehearts: Untold Stories from the Indian Army by General Satish Dua, Juggernaut Books, 2020.

Chapter 17

Nazir's Last Roar

2018, the Last Year

Nazir Wani was an intense family man who was extremely proud of his two sons. It was his fervent desire that his sons not have to make the choices that he had to make during his childhood. The boys were growing up. Athar was in his final year of school and would soon prepare to become an engineer. Shahid was already a teenager. They had planned his admission to a coaching institution in Kota, Rajasthan, to prepare him for a medical college entrance exam. There were several students from Kashmir pursuing studies in Kota. Nazir and his family also had plans to progress with the construction of their house in Jammu.

On 18 January 2018, Nazir went on leave. When he returned to his unit in March, he was assigned to another RR Bn affiliated with the Jat Regiment[23] along with Zahoor and Hav. Bashir Ahmed Shah. They were assigned to B Company, deployed in Nohama, Kulgam. This was the first time ever that his unit was changed. But a disciplined soldier never questions. Besides, he was in Kulgam, the area he knew well and where his family was. And that is all that mattered.

He would often say to his wife and friends, 'I think I am tired now. Maybe I will work for two more years and then settle down in Jammu.' He and Mahajabeen had been seriously discussing the possibilities of doing that. He had bought a plot in Jammu and started constructing his house there.

---

[23] It implies that this RR Bn is affiliated with and has fifty percent troops from the Jat Regiment, just like his previous RR Bn is affiliated with the Rajputana Rifles (RAJRIF)

In July–August, he had gone to Kota with his wife to get his younger son, Shahid, admitted to the school that also coaches students for competitive exams. They were to stop in Jammu on their way back. Leaving her younger son in Kota was difficult for Mahajabeen. It was a wrench for both the son and the parents to be parting, but his future hinged on such decisions, and this was the time to make those compromises. While returning, he broke his journey at Delhi on Col P.S. Jamwal's insistence. His meeting with the Colonel and his family was like a reunion. They had so much to recall. Whenever people have shared hardships and especially dangers together, there will be a special bond, and they don't mind repeating the same anecdotes over and over.

During his conversation, Nazir also informed his former Company Commander and CO about his decision to retire and live in Jammu with his family. 'I have already invested in a small house there, Sir. I don't want my children to grow up under the shadow of violence and uncertainty. I don't want them to have to make hard choices the way I had to when I was a teenager.'

Col Jamwal told him that his promotion to the rank of brigadier was due in a couple of years, and he wanted to come to Kashmir as Sector Commander. Nazir promptly replied, 'Yeh toh bahut mubarak alfaaz hain [This is blessed news], Sir. In that case, I will gladly extend my service so that I can be in your QRT once more, Inshallah.' That was the kind of bond they shared, and such was the trust and confidence his superior officers had in him. He also met Maj. Pratik of the Rajputana Rifles (RAJRIF) regiment in Delhi, with whom he had served in the previous RR Bn. Mahajabeen accompanied him to both of these officers' houses, where they had a meal each.

Nazir, Mahajabeen and Athar missed Shahid. His endless playful quarrelling with his Bhaijaan, his mock complaints to his parents and more to his mother, all of it was a distant memory, and there was a void in the house. Mahajabeen would recall even his reckless behaviour of trying to drive the car a couple of times without any driving skills. It used to infuriate her. But now, all she felt was maternal love and longing.

In the middle of September, Nazir was saddened by another tragedy. Nk Mukhtar Ahmed Malik, his long-time friend since his early days in Ikhwan and a fellow soldier in the TA was killed by terrorists. He had gone home on leave when his son died in a road accident. A couple of terrorists killed him during the condolence meeting at his home. It particularly saddened him, as they were from the same place and had joined Ikhwan together when they were in their teens.

November 2018, the Last Month

In early November 2018, Shahid returned from Kota, and it was a joyous reunion for Nazir's family. On 10 November, he left for Kota again. A day prior, he went to meet his father at the camp, spent the better part of the day with him and that was the last time they met. But it was by providence that they met just then, exactly a fortnight before that fateful encounter in which Nazir made the supreme sacrifice.

In November, Nazir applied for leave. The TA soldiers had to apply to the HQ, the 162 Inf Bn TA, which would send a reliever, if possible, while sanctioning the leave. Nazir wanted to go to Kota and also to Jammu to progress with the construction of his house there. So, he applied for leave, which was to be sanctioned by his TA unit HQ. On 24 November 2018, he returned from an area domination patrol (ADP) and was told that the log message sanctioning his leave had been received from his battalion. It was late evening already. He casually said, 'I'll go on 26 November.'

That was not to be. An operation started on the night of 24
November, and it was his dead body that reached home on
26 November.

The Last Roar

A Company Assault Team (CAT) is a team of selected
volunteer soldiers that leads operations and exposes itself to
maximum risk.

Maj. Sachin Andotra, his Company Commander, was very
impressed by Nazir. His reputation preceded him when he got
posted to his new unit. Initially, Sachin was a bit sceptical,
but he soon discovered that Nazir was even better than he
had imagined. He told me that Nazir had such a reassuring
presence that, as Company Commander, he felt that if he were
ever surrounded by terrorists firing at him from all sides,
Nazir would jump in to save him. In June, when Sachin was
going on leave, Capt. Mahesh from E Company came in to
relieve him as Company Commander. As Sachin was leaving,
he told Nazir, '*Sahab ko accha operation dena* [Give Sir the
opportunity to conduct a successful operation].' However, no
encounters with terrorists took place during his leave. It is
worth appreciating the psyche of soldiers. Whether going on
leave or relieving another colleague, all one is thinking of is
how to do a 'successful operation'. It is this singular focus and
zeal that make the Indian Army one of the most professional
armies in the world.

The next time Maj. Sachin went on leave for a few days
in November, it was Mahesh again who was sent to relieve
him as Company Commander because he was familiar with
the men as well as the terrain. While seeing off Sachin, Nazir
asked with easy familiarity born out of camaraderie, 'Sir,
waapis kab aaoge [Sir, when will you return]?' Sachin replied,
'*Bees din ke baad, lekin is baar Sahab ko operation zaroor*

dena [I'll return after twenty days. Make sure Sir has the opportunity to conduct a successful operation this time].'

And he did. What an operation it was!

Operation Batagund, the Last Operation

On 24 November 2018, a tip-off was received that on the *Chahrum* (fourth day of mourning of the dead) of one of the terrorists killed earlier, some terrorists from his group were likely to attend the prayers and condolence meeting. So the 34 RR Bn (JAT) laid an ambush by twelve soldiers; it turned out to be a futile operation. Either the intelligence was wrong or the terrorists had found out about the ambush. These things happen often, and soldiers are quite used to it. The Company Commander called them back to the company operating base (COB) as there was no sign of terrorists.

They had barely finished their dinner when a police party arrived around 11.15 p.m. with the confirmed electronic input of the presence of terrorists in the village of Batagund, Shopian. Nazir spoke to them in Kashmiri too. He turned towards Capt. Mahesh and said with a slight smile, 'Sir, I think today we will go for the operation that Major Sahib has been wanting for you.'

Nazir felt confident that this was actionable intelligence because police inputs were usually reliable. They had a very keen ear to the ground. Mahesh decided they would not use vehicles in order to maintain surprise. They picked up their weapons, checked their ammunition and grenades, and set forth on foot. Grenades form a very important part of a soldier's arsenal during such close-quarter battles. It was pinpoint information about a specific house in Batagund. The cordon was established from one side. Soldiers from D Company were to complete the cordon from the other side. All the soldiers were crawling along the ground so that no movement or sound would alert the terrorists. Thus, their progress was slow. It was a clear night with good visibility, which also impeded speedy progress.

Nazir went around counting everybody and reassuring the soldiers. It had become a habit, as he had been doing this for years. It was particularly useful since he was the Company Commander's buddy. Another column from D Company arrived, but they came in a Casspir (a heavy mine protected vehicle). This gave away the surprise, and the terrorists came to know that the army had surrounded them. One terrorist jumped out of the window. Soldiers started firing. The terrorists returned the favour. A heavy exchange of fire ensued. Capt. Mahesh and Nazir took up position on the likely escape route and bravely held their fire. It is not easy to hold your fire and let the terrorist come closer when there is a lot of firing going on and the terrorist is firing his weapon too. His bullets were not effective, and they were hiding behind cover. Things could be different if the terrorists were also lobbing grenades, as a grenade could be lobbed over a cover. They waited patiently and fired only at point-blank range, and the terrorist was killed.

Ramu Sharma had taken up position in a neighbouring house that was under construction. Nazir crept up and advised him to fire single shots instead of automatic bursts to conserve ammunition. He even advised him to aim and fire from shoulder position rather than unaimed fire from hip position, because one tends to fire in automatic burst mode from the hip and single shot from the shoulder. He then crept away in the night. His presence was so reassuring, recalled Ramu when he was narrating the memory of the encounter to me.

During the exchange of fire, when a soldier got hit by a terrorist's bullet in the right arm, Nazir tried to evacuate him, but he refused, saying it was not serious enough and he could still continue firing, which he did. Nazir then crawled away to a flank and kept firing from his AK rifle at the terrorist. He crept closer and lobbed a grenade at the terrorist. It must have been effective because the firing stopped for a bit and Nazir fired a few long bursts on him or them. As he closed in, it was confirmed that there were two of them as suspected. One had been eliminated by Nazir's volley of bullets, and the other made a dash in the direction of the wounded soldier, who was alert and brought the escaping terrorist down at close range. That was three down.

Suddenly, the firing from inside the house had become less intense. Then it stopped for a bit. When Mahesh and Nazir tried to crawl ahead, they drew fire from a different window. But it was single shots or short bursts. The terrorists were conserving ammunition; having lost three of their colleagues had shown them how effectively they were surrounded, and they were preparing themselves for the long haul. Realizing that other terrorists would not escape this way, where two of them had been brought down, Mahesh and Nazir changed their position.

They crawled cautiously to the rear of the house. Assessing the situation, there appeared to be one likely route of escape, and Mahesh asked Nazir to cover that street. He himself moved around fifteen to twenty yards to the side, from where he could observe the rear of the house as well as the broad side of the house. Mahesh and Nazir were in visual communication, or *nazari milap*, as it is called in the army. Buddies are supposed to deploy together or can separate slightly, if required, but should be in supporting distance and communication.

This redeployment paid dividends, because soon shots were heard from the rear of the house. Mahesh and Nazir held their fire to maintain surprise. A few shots were fired back from the cordon party, which was behind the houses to the rear, at a little distance. Suddenly, without any warning, there was a volley of shots from the house in their direction, accompanied by a grenade explosion. They both ducked behind cover. Nazir anticipated that if someone has to escape, it will be after lobbing a grenade, so he cautiously peered around the cover. Sure enough, one of them darted out of the house with his weapon blazing, and the fire intensified to the side, towards Company Commander Capt. Mahesh. As the fleeing terrorist rushed out, Nazir displayed nerves of steel and held his fire until he was very close to his right. Calmly, he fired a short burst, which stopped the running man in his tracks. Four down.

A fire seemed to have broken out in the house, as they could see the flames from a window. Something may have caught fire during the exchange of fire. Or had the terrorists lit the fire themselves? What were they up to?

It was 5 a.m., and the house was still not free from terrorists. Soon it would be time for Azaan (the chanting of morning prayers) in the mosque, and it would be daylight shortly thereafter. Not that the neighbours would be sleeping now, but there is also the risk of crowds gathering to pelt stones at the soldiers in the cordon parties. Such are the pressures and tensions that play on soldiers' minds while operating in counter-terrorist operations.

They called the house owner and asked him to go inside and see if there were more terrorists hiding inside. Terrorists usually do not kill civilians or members of the household; otherwise, they will not get shelter in any house. So, the owner went inside cautiously, trying to keep himself safe from the portion that was on fire. He returned a few minutes later, coughing and sputtering. He pointed with his index finger held up, signalling that one terrorist was still inside. As it turned out, he was a hardcore foreign terrorist by the name of Ali who was involved in several brutal killings. The house owner told Nazir that he had wrapped himself in a wet quilt to be safe from the flames. It also turned out that there were two terrorists and not one, inside the house, but the house owner did not know that.

Capt. Mahesh, the stand-in Company Commander, was eager to wrap up the operation as it was already daylight. He beckoned to Nazir and began crawling forward. Nazir took the protective shield from Mushtaq, but as he started moving forward, he found it heavy and cumbersome. So, he handed the shield back to Mushtaq. Capt. Mahesh and Nazir crept up to the room, and Mushtaq and his buddy followed close behind. There was plenty of smoke and heat; the fire was perhaps bigger than it seemed from outside. Mahesh signalled to Nazir to move to the other side of the entrance door. Nazir lost his patience and moved past him, or rather charged, into the room, his assault rifle blazing. Combat fatigue can do that to you. They had been exchanging fire and wits the whole night, after all.

The terrorist was trying to escape through a window. Nazir lunged at him, and they were locked in a hand-to-hand fight. There was too much smoke, dust and explosive noise. The terrorist had fallen. But Nazir was also hit. Before Mahesh could react, another terrorist fired from the corner of the room, hiding behind a table under which things were piled up. Mahesh dropped to the ground and fired a burst through the heat and smoke. The firing ceased. The last terrorist was down.

Capt. Mahesh crawled over to Nazir. He lay unmoving. He was absolutely still. He had sustained gunshot wounds to his face. It was a bloody mess. It was all over.

Capt. Mahesh came out shaken and dumbfounded. On repeated asking, he told Mushtaq Ahmad that Nazir was no more. Mushtaq could not believe it. Nobody could. There was a sense of utter disbelief. They had all gotten so used to being around Nazir's reassuring and energizing presence. A pall of gloom descended on his battalion. All ranks had become used to his enthusiasm and steadying influence in operations. He was soft-spoken yet self-assured.

Ab Bacha Hi Kya Hai? It's All Over . . .

Mushtaq ruefully recalls that while going in for the final search, Capt. Mahesh was carrying a bulletproof shield. Nazir had briefly taken a similar shield from Mushtaq, mumbled something about it being too heavy and handed it back to him. Had he become complacent, or was it that his time had come?

Maj. Sachin Andotra, his Company Commander, who was on leave when this operation took place, later recalled how he read about the operation at home and was overwhelmed at Nazir's supreme self-sacrifice. The motivation hall in his B Company was named 'Nazir Hall', in which details and pictures of major operations are displayed. While the officers and soldiers in the RR battalions change every two to three years, this motivation hall would always remind everyone of Nazir's bravery to inspire the newly inducted soldiers.

Nazir was unparalleled in operations. Absolutely fearless. He was also unflappable under pressure, which had a calming influence on others. He had a good and cordial rapport with everyone, including civilians. Sushil told me later what a calming influence and reassuring feeling he exuded whenever he was with his colleagues. When Sushil was posted to the unit, Nazir was one of the first people he met, and over time, he became deeply influenced by Nazir's fearlessness. It was infectious. '*Uske saath rah kar hamara bhi darr nikal gaya* [Being with him got rid of my fear too],' he said with a smile.

Sometimes, when they were together, they would act mute and use sign language. Nazir strongly believed that if you spoke less, you would make fewer mistakes.

When I asked him to reminisce more, he recalled other interesting aspects about Nazir. Whenever the soldiers were standing and eating, he would chide them, saying, '*Baith ke khao, chain se raho* [Sit down and eat peacefully].' Whenever he returned from a trip to his home, he would always bring a dish or two for his colleagues to eat, sometimes milk or sometimes kadam ka saag. Maj. Sachin, his Company Commander, also recalled that once he asked him, '*Aapne kabhi kadam wali fish curry khayi hai*? [Have you ever tasted fish curry prepared with kadam]?' When he returned from home the next day, he brought a really tasty local fish preparation made with kadam, which is an underground bulb with delicious leaves overground and is used in several Kashmiri recipes. These thoughtful little gestures endeared him to everyone.

I asked his wife, Mahajabeen, if they ever quarreled. She replied that it was very difficult to get angry with Nazir. He was always so positive and helpful that she rarely lost her cool. On the odd occasion when she did, it was also impossible to sustain the anger for long with him. In fact, the only time she felt annoyed was once he was going through the town with the CO, Col Jamwal, and she felt Nazir was ignoring her. Besides these little episodes, she felt hers was a fulfilling and happy married life.

Chapter 18

Soldiering Continues

Less than four weeks after I hung up my boots, I heard of the supreme sacrifice of L/Nk Nazir Ahmed Wani. Only a few months earlier, as Colonel of the JAKLI regiment, I had sent my felicitations to him for being awarded a Bar to Sena Medal, euphemism for a second Sena Medal for gallantry. On Republic Day in 2019, I felt proud when I heard the news that Nazir was awarded the highest gallantry award, the Ashok Chakra, posthumously. I went and met his parents, wife and son, who had come to receive the highest medal of bravery from the President during the Republic Day Parade as a grateful nation watched and clapped with pride and tears.

I wish to end with a thought that has bothered me for years. I was colonel of the JAKLI Regiment while I was Corps Commander in Srinagar and chief of the Integrated Defence Staff. There were a couple of incidents in which JAKLI soldiers' families were roughed up by their neighbours; in one case, their house was burned down by the terrorist or separatist elements. Sons of the soil often face these challenges. I had set up a helpline in the RR battalions and the JAKLI Regimental Centre to assist families when they faced such problems while their husbands were serving in other places. We had the case of the kidnapping and killing by terrorists of Rfn Aurangzeb of my regiment whose last video, a few minutes before the terrorists killed him, inspired the nation as he looked calmly into the eyes of the terrorists and said he was not afraid to die. There was no begging, no groveling. Nk Mukhtar of the JAKLI TA was killed by terrorists when he had gone home for the funeral of his son. Lt Umar Fayyaz, though not from

JAKLI, was killed by terrorists when he was on leave to attend a family wedding.

On the other hand, I have often heard from other regimental officers, including COs, about an element of mistrust that creeps in when some senior officers begin to doubt the loyalty of JAKLI soldiers, especially Kashmiri Muslims. It pains me to hear of such sentiments when I can vouch for the bravery of these men. This mistrust increased after the Aurangzeb kidnapping incident in 2017, when it was established that the terrorists were alerted by another soldier of his unit about the vehicle he was travelling in.

There was an attack at Sanjuwan Cantt in Jammu, where a JAKLI battalion was also deployed, among others, in 2018. Doubts were raised that the involvement of some soldiers and their families could not be ruled out. Some senior officers even began to question the reverses suffered by a JAKLI battalion on the LoC in Rajauri Sector.

I visited both of these units after the incidents as Colonel of the Regiment and met several senior officers in the chain of command as well.

Almost all senior officers have served in J&K at different levels. They are hostages to their own impressions. In my view, some of them carry forward a distorted assessment, which makes it difficult for them to differentiate between a Kashmiri Muslim soldier and a Kashmiri terrorist, though the number of such officers is small. There is a significant difference; it lies in upbringing, the environment and exposure. A young boy who is radicalized and misguided is going to be easy prey for militancy and terrorism. On the other hand, a teenager who becomes a soldier is put through rigorous training, imbued with a spirit of duty and camaraderie and above all, removed from this environment of hatred and violence. He serves in different parts of the country. This serves two purposes. One, it removes him from the disruptive atmosphere of day-to-day strife and negativity, and secondly, he gets an opportunity to see the rest of the country and see how much better things are when bereft of violence and strife. This is what makes the difference in the mind of a soldier.

Some Sikh battalions revolted during the Punjab problem years, yet Sikhs are at the cutting edge in the army. There are Baloch rebels in Pakistan, yet the Baloch Regiment is the Pakistan Army's pride. We need to see J&K soldiers in that spirit. Those belonging to border areas have their own challenges and compulsions, which we all must endeavour to comprehend. It must also be appreciated that these sons of the soil, the Kashmiri Muslims, are the only soldiers who are operationally deployed in their home region, because of which they and their families face constant threats and persecution. Some of them, such as this TA Battalion and the Ikhwan earlier, are permanently deployed in their home state and always remain in operations. They add a lot of value to their unit's intelligence and operational quotient—at great risk to themselves. No one can deny that we were able to conduct the assembly election in 1996 primarily because of Ikhwan. And that election was a turning point in the political saga of Kashmir.

The JAKLI soldiers are found in the QRTs of each CO and each Company Commander in the RR units.

Scores of JAKLI soldiers have made the supreme sacrifice, whether on the LoC or in the fight against militancy. But some twisted minds have doubted their patriotism, thus exposing them to constant barbs, threats and friction. However, the hundreds of medals and awards conferred on them by a grateful nation are the true testimony to their bravery and dedication.

I have always been trying to explain to the Kashmiri youth that every soldier with an AK rifle is not an enemy, and I wish every soldier and army officer understood that every Kashmiri Muslim with a beard is not a terrorist.

Epilogue

Life After Article 370

An epilogue is apt here, as so far it has been a duologue between Nazir's saga of valour and my impressions of J&K over the decades.

Less than a year after Nazir's supreme sacrifice, on 5 August 2019, the Indian Parliament passed an amendment modifying Article 370, which defined the special constitutional status of the erstwhile state of Jammu and Kashmir. It also abrogated Article 35A, which empowered the J&K State Legislature to define its permanent residents. The state of J&K defined these privileges to include the ability to purchase land and immovable property, the ability to vote and contest elections, seeking government employment and availing oneself of other state benefits, such as higher education and healthcare.

Moreover, the state of J&K was also bifurcated into two union territories: the union territories of Jammu-Kashmir (with a legislature) and Ladakh (without a legislature). It has been an epic and bold decision, long overdue.

From a security perspective, the whittling down of Article 370 in J&K was a welcome step. Security concerns could be addressed better than before without local pressure. The UN response had been cautious while making the expected diplomatic observations. The US and most other countries

175

have, by and large, taken the position that it is an internal matter and that any differences must be resolved through peaceful dialogue. This move took Pakistan completely by surprise, and they were somewhat at a loss for words. However, Pakistan had no choice; it had to express solidarity with Kashmir. Kashmir is the glue that binds their country together and enshrines the central role of the Pakistani Army in their country. Pakistan has therefore, as expected, snapped trade and diplomatic ties with India.

In the intervening years, the J&K administration has undertaken an all-government approach to create a secure and stable environment, prosecute development, dispense good and fair administration and generate outreach. It also empowered grassroots democracy by conducting panchayat elections. For the first time, block development officers were elected, and the District Development Council was formed to realize the aspirations of the people. Grassroots politics has been empowered in J&K for the first time, in keeping with the political aspirations of the people. With efforts to usher in economic activity that meets their aspirations, the endeavour is to create an environment to start the political process at the state level as soon as possible.

The administration of the union territory has instituted several measures of development since the marginalization of Article 370. In the last few years, 100 per cent electrification has taken place, and surpassing the national average, 53 per cent of rural areas have drinking water supply. Fifteen power projects have been inaugurated, and twenty more have been started. The new All India Institute of Medical Sciences, Indian Institute of Technology, Indian Institute of Management, and about fifty other new educational institutions will benefit 25,000 additional students. Grassroots-level politics has also been empowered by putting a three-tier panchayat in place. Approximately Rs 3800 crore has been allocated through this route to meet local aspirations.

Meeting the growth aspirations of the youth, as anywhere else, cannot be done by government jobs or the public sector alone; it needs private sector participation. In the last four years, the private sector has stepped up in J&K, which was hitherto rather limited. Investment proposals worth Rs 20,000 crore have been received from forty private sector companies in fields such as IT, defence, renewable energy, tourism, hospitality, education and infrastructure. Two huge IT parks are being set up in Jammu and Srinagar, respectively.

One also gathers that some corporate hospitals are stepping into healthcare in J&K. The people of Kashmir have started enjoying the pleasure of a multiplex in Srinagar (all cinema halls were banned by terrorists and separatists earlier). Eateries such as Pizza Hut, Haldiram and Nathu Sweets have set up shop, and the Emaar group of Burj Khalifa fame has constructed a huge mall. Thirty-nine MOUs have also been signed with real estate biggies.[24] We should soon see BPOs and call centres in the Valley.

This goes to show that the youth of Kashmir are increasingly going to enjoy facilities and services that they have only been seeing in movies, on the Internet and on YouTube. Youth anywhere have similar aspirations. However, it will not be correct to say that everyone is happy and there is no alienation. There are a significant number that remain alienated, even radicalized. There is widespread resentment towards downgrading the state to a union territory. The other side has also been active in adapting to changing circumstances. The number of terrorists operating in the Valley is in the region of around a hundred, compared to thousands in the 1990s. They are also poorly trained, if at all.

[24] IANS, 'Real Estate MoUs to Haldiram, Industrial Development in J&K Gets a Boost', *Business Standard*, December 27, 2021, https://www.business-standard.com/article/current-affairs/real-estate-mous-to-haldiram-industrial-development-in-j-k-gets-a-boost-121122700352_1.html.

The strong anti-infiltration grid on the LoC does not allow them to exfiltrate to POK to be trained in terrorist training camps. Therefore, the other side has started relying on the use of social media as a force multiplier for mobilization as well as the radicalization of youth. This is information warfare. The battlefield is shifting to the mindspace of the youth rather than remaining confined to the jungles and mountains only. Our approach must also change accordingly. First, we must recognize this change and focus on information warfare by itself and not as an adjunct to kinetic operations.

The state needs to build a narrative around the positives. The other side, the 'Deep State' has built a narrative on hate and negativity. They've radicalized the youth, by preying on the fears of people and made false promises, whether it's to do with jannat (heaven) and hoors (virgins) or better days in Pakistan or azadi (freedom). A national narrative should be created around the tangible positives: jobs, opportunities, industry, good administration, grass-roots empowerment and recreational outlets such as sports and cultural enrichment. It is easy to draw a contrast between the failed state of affairs in Pakistan and the economic growth and the rising importance of India in the world. I had written an article on this topic in the Quint in January 2022.[25]

After the dilution of Article 370, a few new terror groups have emerged. With names like The Resistance Front (TRF), People's Anti-Fascist Front (PAFF) and United Liberation Front (ULF), they sound more liberal and less fundamentalist. They are essentially a front for LET, JEM and other groups. It serves the purpose of circumventing Financial Action Task Force (FATF) compliance for Pakistan by cutting off funding

---

[25] Lt Gen Satish Dua, 'India's Kashmir Outreach Must Focus On Winning the Youth's Trust', Quint, January 28, 2022, https://www.thequint.com/opinion/indias-kashmir-outreach-must-focus-on-winning-the-youths-trust#read-more.

to terrorist groups. These groups also have a strong online presence, taking a leaf out of the playbook of the Islamic State in Iraq and Syria (ISIS), the dreaded terrorist organization in the Middle East.

The latest entrant in this changing face of terrorism in Kashmir is the hybrid terrorist. This poses a bigger challenge for the security forces, as the terrorist is overtly a part of society. However, he is radicalized, alienated or both. He is not formally trained in the use of weapons. But it does not require too much training or practice to use a pistol or a grenade. These hybrid terrorists carry out targeted killings of soft targets to instill fear in the minds of the people. They carry out one such incident of violence and merge back into society. The other side wants to disrupt the feel-good sentiment in the populace that things are going back towards normalcy. Thus, there is a need to involve civil society in a more meaningful way. The common man in Kashmir is also fed up with violence. It is time to put all instruments in play to get the saner part of society to come forward to help themselves. The successful drive by the National Intelligence Agency (NIA) and Enforcement Directorate (ED) to target the fund flow of those who instigate violence, the overground workers and other middle-level managers is paying good dividends.

Whenever the time is right, the details should be exposed to the public, whom they exploit.

However, in addition to the growth opportunities, some other intangible steps are needed to erode the alienation amongst youth and provide a healing touch to the people and the civil society, especially the youth.

For two main reasons, the requirement to connect with the mind space of youth is imperative. First, it is youth that will shape tomorrow's opinions and attitudes. Second, it is very difficult to change the mindset and attitude of the older generation. We need constructive engagement with the youth and the children. And use the narrative to counter alienation and radicalization as well. We must get back into the minds of the youth. Youth are the key to integration. The idea of azadi must be supplanted by the idea of India.

In order to connect with the mindspace of the people, it is imperative that the state put out a coordinated and credible narrative based on truth. There have been shortcomings in building a good narrative, a space that was quickly filled up by the other side with a narrative of hate. There is an urgent need to reverse it. This strategic communication is needed to dispel uncertainty and the fear of the future from the minds of the people and create hope in their minds.

The winning of hearts and minds and constructive engagement with the *awaam* (general public) is something that the Indian Army engages in through the medium of Operation Sadbhavna (goodwill). While there is scope for the other organs of the government and even the private sector to follow suit, this is by no means enough in itself.

A change in approach is warranted as far as dealing with youth is concerned. They are misled by vested interests. A healing touch is the need of the hour. During encounters with terrorists, the army always gives the terrorists a chance to surrender, and several of them have taken advantage of the opportunity. Similarly, the security forces, including the police, should engage with the stone pelters and their families as well. They should be treated like our misguided children, something that I often said when I was the Corps Commander in Kashmir. Prolonged interrogation of the errant youth and their families leads to alienation, and Pakistan's ISI has its minions on the watch for such candidates; they reach out to such young men and their families with financial assistance and moral support to draw them into militancy.

States such as Maharashtra and Kerala have successfully used de-radicalization as a counter-terrorism strategy. It's time we followed the example of the Maharashtra Anti-Terrorism Squad, which has been able to pull many youngsters back from the edge. According to Maharashtra Deputy Commissioner of Police Dhananjay Kulkarni, in a dated report, the three-year-old de-radicalization programme has 'reintegrated' at least 114 young men and six women who were being wooed by ISIS. The policemen who turned counsellors in the ATS also counselled 200 others.[26] Youth in Jammu and Kashmir also need such a healing touch.

The civil society has an important role to play as well. They need to stand up to the hate mongers who incite their children to take the wrong path while their own children and wards are prospering in safe locales outside of J&K or even the country. Whether it was Punjab or Mizoram, terrorism could only be contained with the active assistance of civil society. There is a great potential waiting to be unlocked in Kashmiri civil society. This assumes all the more importance with the latest trend of hybrid terrorists, who live within society and indulge in targeted killings of soft targets.

It will not happen in a hurry. It will take up to a generation or two to affect mindset changes. We have to be patient. As a union territory to be administered by the Centre, the Union government must ensure that this change leads to a better state of affairs in all aspects, bringing the people together. This will preclude Pakistan from exploiting the situation to their advantage.

What is the way forward to move towards state elections? Terrorist violence has been fairly under control during the year gone by. The incidence of mob violence and stone-pelting has also been very low, compared to earlier times. Even despite the dilution of Article 370 or detentions, there has

[26] Sagar Rajput, 'Maharashtra ATS's Deradicalisation Programme: "I Realised Allah Didn't Want Me to Sacrifice My Life to Make Him Happy"', *Indian Express*, August 1, 2019, https://indianexpress.com/article/india/maharashtra-ats-deradicalisation-programme-muslim-youth-is-recruit-allah-didnt-want-me-to-sacrifice-my-life-5868100/.

been comparatively less spilling of anger on the streets. A huge exercise in the fresh delimitation of electoral constituencies has been carried out after decades. As soon as the time is right, the political process at the state level should resume, and the upgradation of the union territory to a state must follow.

Here, I will stick my neck out to make a bold suggestion. Is it also time to articulate an exit strategy for the army in J&K? Let me explain. As the situation in the LoC and hinterland gets better, should we think of how to repurpose the army's involvement in J&K? On the one hand, the army's presence and reach in the remotest areas and its organizational strength can be leveraged for the greater good of coordinating information warfare and the psychological dimension.

On the hard kinetics front, should we articulate an exit strategy for the army? Imagine that the army returns to its barracks and hands over the day-to-day security operations to the J&K Police and the CRPF. The army can remain in a hand-holding role and continue to underwrite peace by remaining in their hubs and bases in case the situation turns ugly. It can also help in training and intelligence gathering. But day-to-day operations and the protection of roads and installations can be handed over to the CRPF and the police. This will leave the army free to conduct information warfare and target the mind space of the youth. When this can actually take place depends on the improvement in the situation.

This transition cannot happen in a hurry, but merely by articulating it, we will create more stakeholders in the peace process. Today, sadly, every aspect of the situation in Kashmir seems to be outsourced to the army.

The army will, however, continue to be deployed on the LoC to secure the borders as well as the anti-infiltration grid. If anything, it will get reinforced where required. This grid had to be made as foolproof as possible in view of the fact

that more terrorists are likely to be available to Pakistan as
the situation in Afghanistan becomes more volatile due to the
withdrawal of American troops.

To end, I would like to highlight a couple of thoughts,
even at the expense of repetition. The state of affairs in the
union territory of J&K has improved tremendously. There
are no bandhs, no strikes, no school closures, no violence
spilling on the streets and no stone-pelting worth mentioning.
There is peace and development to a great degree, and it is
growing. Tourists are thronging to the Valley, which provides
employment to lakhs of people. An international meeting of
the G-20 on tourism was held successfully, showcasing all of
this to delegates from across the world.

However, all our troubles are not yet over. The other
side will continue to change tactics. Just before going to the
press, there has been a spate of terrorist attacks in the Jammu
region in mid 2024. It is clearly the terrorists' response to
the peaceful conduct of parliamentary elections in J&K
on the back of the improvement of the situation. Their
endeavour is to activate the dormant areas and instill fear in
the minds of the people.

However, the state must prevail by adapting to the new
realities. We must ensure that the violence is curbed by all
of the government and security forces approach, including
intelligence agencies. The army has already augmented its
deployment and attendant actions are underway. And above
all, the state elections must be held as planned, thereby
defeating the terrorists' designs and that of their handlers
from across the LoC.

The political process must start as soon as possible, giving
expression to the political aspirations of the populace. A
return to statehood can also follow. For this, civil society must
be strengthened to participate and be more responsive and
responsible. Only these sons of the soil can bring about lasting

solutions. We saw their brave stand against the invaders from Pakistan in 1947, when volunteer groups that later formed my regiment, the Jammu and Kashmir Militia, stood up to fight the invaders. In controlling the terrorist violence, we saw these sons of the soil in Ikhwan, which marked the turn-around in the mid-1990s, and their later avatar, the TA Battalion of JAKLI, of which Nazir Wani and his ilk were a part. So, for every Burhan Wani, there were many Nazir Wanis, Aurangzebs and more to fight for humanity in Kashmir, to make it the Jannat that it once was. Kashmiri Muslims are one of the rare sons of the soil in India who have been employed in operations in an insurgency against their own.

For all the sacrifices made and all the sufferings, it is only right that the younger generation of J&K gets to live in a jannat, as it has traditionally been called. And the world too gets to see it as only that—a heaven on earth. To end with these words of the great Amir Khusro: '*Gar Firdaus bar roo-e zameen ast, hameen ast-o, hameen ast-o, hameen ast.*'

(If there is heaven on earth, it is here, it is here, it is here.)

Acknowledgements

My father would always urge me to write a book, even when I was busy soldiering. Just like my first book, this one is also for you, Dad. You have always been my role model. I seek the blessings of Sri Aurobindo and the Divine Mother for this book as well as for everything else.

I want to acknowledge the role of my wife, Aradhana, and my sons, Adamya and Ardaman, who put up with my absence from home for years at a stretch, owing to my deployments in operational areas, based on which this book is written.

To piece together the story of Nazir Ahmed Wani, this son of the soil, the terrorist turned Ikhwan turned soldier turned hero, I travelled widely in Central and South Kashmir after my retirement and interviewed scores of people from Nazir's family, friends, colleagues from Ikhwan and TA days, also RR units, with whom he operated, and also his superior officers in the RR and TA units. It may not be possible to acknowledge everyone by name, but I would like to thank the more prominent ones, and several of the rest appear in the narrative. I wish to begin by profusely thanking the parents and wife, Mahajabeen, of L/Nk Nazir Ahmad Wani, his close buddies L/Nk Zahoor Ahmed and L/Nk Mushtaq Ahmed Mir aka Maulvi, and L/Nk Aijaz Ahmed Rather, the brother-in-law of Nazir, for not only their insights but also for travelling with me to different units and villages in Kashmir for that, including the site where Nazir made the supreme sacrifice.

I thank surrendered terrorist leaders such as Sheikh Tahir, Romeo aka Subedar Mushtaq Ahmed Bhatt, and Liaqat Ali; not all of them are from the 162 Inf TA Bn (H&H). I met them all in Anantnag, Kulgam and other parts of Kashmir. My grateful thanks to all the army officers who had operated with Nazir in the Rashtriya Rifles, the most notable among them being Col P.S. Jamwal, Maj. Sachin Andotra, Capt. Mahesh and Col Sudhir Tiwari, who raised and commanded this bold experiment called the 162 Inf Bn TA (H&H), gave me a very good understanding of the various intricacies of the birth of this battalion and its dynamics when I travelled to Lucknow to meet with him. I also spoke to several senior army officers to get a good understanding of the Ikhwan and TA days; notable among them were the former Eastern Army Commander Lt Gen. Rana Kalita and Brig. Ajay Kumar, a retired course mate of mine.

My gratitude goes to two of my friends, Col Anil Nayer and Gopi Gopalkrishnan, who read every word of the manuscript and made valuable suggestions.

I also warmly thank my publisher and editor, Milee Aishwarya, for her expert guidance through the writing of this book. I also express my gratitude for the team at Penguin Random House India comprising Peter Modoli, Ahana Singh, Aishvarya Misra, Naina Tripathi, Sparsh Raj Singh and Yash Daiv.

Finally, I thank all my mentors and superiors, the brave officers and soldiers that I have been fortunate to command, not only in my Bravest of the Brave Battalion, 8 JAKLI (Siachen), but also beyond, throughout my career, for I have learned something from everyone.

I also thank the reader for being a part of this journey now. Jai Hind!

Glossary of Military Terms Used in the Book

JAKLI - Jammu and Kashmir Light Infantry
TA - Territorial Army
RR - Rashtriya Rifles
Bn - Battalion
COB - Company Operating Base
JCO - Junior Commissioned Officer
NCO - Non-Commissioned Officer
POK - Pakistan Occupied Kashmir
LoC - Line of Control
MUF - Muslim United Front
FT - Foreign terrorists
UBGL - Under Barrel Grenade Launcher
MMG - Medium Machine Gun
LMG - Light Machine Gun
BPP - Bulletproof Patka
QRT - Quick Reaction Team
MoD - Ministry of Defence
UAV - Unarmed Aerial Vehicles
IED - Improvised Explosive Device
ALH - Advanced Landing Helicopter

Scan QR code to access the
Penguin Random House India website